With Knife & Fork Around the Globe

Mags Pie

Published by Mags Pie, 2023.

While every precaution has been taken in the preparation of this book, the publisher assumes no responsibility for errors or omissions, or for damages resulting from the use of the information contained herein.

WITH KNIFE & FORK AROUND THE GLOBE

First edition. August 1, 2023.

Copyright © 2023 Mags Pie.

ISBN: 979-8223299165

Written by Mags Pie.

With Knife and Fork around the Globe

Mags Pie

Disclaimer

THIS FOLLOWING NON-fictional book is intended to provide information and insights based on the available knowledge and research. This book is designed to present general knowledge and perspectives on the topic. It is not intended to replace professional advice.

Finally, the reader understands that this book is protected by copyright laws and unauthorized reproduction, distribution, or transmission of any part of this book, in any form or by any means, without the prior written permission of the author(s) or publisher, is strictly prohibited. By reading this book, the reader acknowledges and agrees to the terms and conditions stated in this disclaimer.

# INTRODUCTION

INTRODUCTION

In this culinary travel guide, we invite you to embark on a delectable journey across 17 captivating gastronomic destinations, where rich histories, vibrant cultures, and diverse gastronomic traditions converge. Get ready to tantalize your taste buds with an array of mouthwatering delicacies, savor traditional recipes passed down through generations, and explore the hidden gems of world's culinary landscape.

From the sun-kissed shores of Spain to the charming countryside of France, the picturesque landscapes of Italy to the cozy tavernas of Greece, each country offers a unique tapestry of flavors, aromas, and culinary experiences. Whether you're a passionate foodie, a curious traveler, or simply someone who appreciates the art of fine dining, this guide promises to awaken your senses and ignite your wanderlust.

Join us as we traverse the winding cobblestone streets of Lisbon, where you'll indulge in freshly caught seafood and sip on Portugal's famous Port wine. Immerse yourself in the romance of Paris, sampling delicate pastries, sipping aromatic wines, and savoring the finest cheeses. Discover the hearty and robust cuisine of Germany, with its sausages, pretzels, and rich stews, or venture into the land of majestic castles and fairy tales in Austria, where you'll experience the delights of Wiener Schnitzel and world-renowned Viennese coffee.

As we cross borders, we'll delve into the timeless culinary traditions of Switzerland, Belgium, and the Netherlands. Sample creamy Swiss chocolates, indulge in decadent Belgian waffles, and savor the famous Dutch cheese. Journey through the flavors of the Balkans, where the simplicity of Bulgarian meatballs and the opulence of the Ottoman cuisine will captivate your palate.

Prepare for a voyage filled with culinary delights, as we explore the Tzar's treasures of Russia. From caviar to blini and Beef Stroganoff, you'll uncover the diverse and hearty flavors that have shaped the region.

Each chapter of this guide will take you on an immersive journey, uncovering local food markets, traditional recipes, renowned restaurants, and even cooking classes where you can master the art of European cuisine yourself. Along the way, you'll discover the stories behind the dishes, the cultural significance of each bite, and the fascinating histories that have shaped these gastronomic wonders.

GREECE, MEDITERRANEAN CORE ADVENTURE

What we call time is a moving unreal reflection of Eternity.
- Plato (427 - 345 BC)

Near and far, ancient and eternal, wise and cheerful, Hellas awaits you with an azure blue, in which the border between the sky and the sea is lost in the infinity of the horizon, with centuries-old olive groves and warm evenings in the company of poets, sages and philosophers. A true adventure of culinary anthropology, peppered with well-kept secrets, fun discoveries and hide and seek in the shadows of similarities and differences. Therefore, Yassou, let's go - no matter if along the vertical of time, along the incised curve of history or along the horizontal of east and west, all roads lead to...

Ancient Greece

Apart from epic wars, bloodthirsty tyrants and wise rulers, great philosophers and tempting beauties, the history of Ancient Hellas is marked by the eternal human pursuit of happiness and prosperity. Ancient literature and visual art abound with evidence of the daily life of the ancient Greeks, of their habits, clothing and food, etiquette and manners. The simple, economical dishes of the demos went with "the best spice - hunger," as Socrates says... For breakfast - bread soaked in wine, for lunch - bread soaked in wine, with a few olives, figs or goat cheese for the lucky ones, for dinner fresh fruit, vegetables and fish, bread, wine and honey. At once it becomes clear that classical ancient cuisine was based on three main products - wheat, olive oil and wine. Not necessarily in that order, as we know from the cult of Dionysius...

Always have a new book in your library, a full barrel in the cellar, a fresh flower in the garden.
Epicurus (341 - 270 BC)

The ancient Greeks revered wine as a divine drink, gifted to them by the god Dionysius. Legend has it that Dionysius was born from the union between the Father of the Gods Zeus and the mortal Semele. Jealous Hera ordered Dionysius to be killed, and when her plan finally succeeded, the goddess Athena created the first vine from his still-beating heart. Therefore, the ancient Greeks believed that drinking wine brought them closer to the gods. They produced white, red and rosé wine of varying quality, from unpretentious home wine for the common people to "vintage" vintages with guaranteed origin and authenticity, special permits and controls, as evidenced by the seals on the found amphorae. The wine was drunk diluted with water, and its effects on both sexes were duly described. But only in Sparta did women drink wine openly. Drinking undiluted wine was believed to lead to insanity, so it was considered barbaric...

Kikeon (Κυκεών) was another popular drink made from roasted barley flour, honey water and fresh mint.

The antique soiree

When it comes to wine, we must mention the tradition of the Greek symposium (συμπόσιον) or literally "drinking with friends". A classic evening gathering where men stretched out on comfortable couches and garlanded with flowers indulged in hymns in honor of Dionysius and mostly intellectual conversation and libations in the company of beautiful Hetairas. Here guests expressed their views on various issues, made new acquaintances and exchanged ideas, as described by Plutarch.

Syssitia (τὰ συσσίτια), on the other hand, was a practically obligatory communal meal for citizens, popular especially in Sparta and on the island of Crete. Again, a predominantly male occupation, although there is historical evidence of female syssitias. At these gatherings, important religious and social issues were discussed, warring clans were reconciled and harmony and peace were restored in the community.

On the trail of culinary influences or the ancient roots of fusion cuisine

By 350 BC, when Alexander the Great had already conquered Macedonia and the Balkans, Achaemenid Persia, Egypt and his state stretched from Greece to present-day Afghanistan, Pakistan and India, Hellenic cuisine was saturated with various northern and eastern influences . But it not only absorbs, but also enriches the culinary traditions of Europe, North Africa and the Middle East.

The first cookbook was written by the forefather of gourmet chefs, Archestratus, in 330 BC. A century later, Athenaeus produced the 15-volume masterpiece Deipnosophistai (Δειπνοσοφισταί), "A Feast for Sophists." In addition to the detailed descriptions of ancient foods and culinary techniques, Athenaeus introduces us to the etiquette and menu of the feasts of that era, introducing the reader to the home of the pontiff Larensius and his 29 guests, who talk about the traditions, daily life, art and science of Ancient Hellas.

In 146 BC Greece became part of the Roman state, and Greek cuisine was enriched with the cooking techniques of the Romans.

In 330, Emperor Constantine moved the capital of the Roman Empire to Constantinople, founding the Byzantine Empire, which in turn was conquered by the Ottomans in 1453, and remained part of the Ottoman Empire for nearly 400 years. Famous Greek dishes acquired Turkish names that remain to this day as the names of many Greek classic feasts. It is not difficult to find the connection between the popular *mezedes* - htapodi (small pieces of grilled octopus, with lemon juice, olive oil and oregano), kalamarakia (fried squid rings with lemon juice), tiropitakia and spanakopitakia (patties with cheese and spinach), melitsanosalata (that is, köpoolu), taramasalata (whipped caviar), tzatziki milk salad and its Turkish version cacik, hummus, that is chickpeas in Arabic, Greek dolmadas (from the Turkish word dolma) or, in other words, miniature vine salad - these are all dishes, which can be found in the national cuisines from Armenia to Egypt without skipping the Balkans.

Modern bosses owe the tradition of tall white hats to none other than the Greeks. During the Middle Ages, the monks who prepared the food in the cloisters of the Greek Orthodox monasteries wore precisely such tall white hats to distinguish themselves from the rest of the brothers with their black carpets.

Cheese 6 thousand years old... According to historians, the production and use of cheese in Greek cuisine dates back to 4th millennium BC. The oldest known cheeses in the world are feta and kasseri.

Let's not forget Aphrodite...

EVERYONE KNOWS THAT an aphrodisiac, by definition a substance (herb or food) that induces or enhances sexual desire, is named after the Greek goddess of love and beauty, Aphrodite. Since ancient times, people have credited certain foods with the ability to increase sexual power and desire, and historical records testify that the ancient Greeks were not immune to promises of brilliant performance, impressive endurance and unearthly delight in love affairs. The father of medicine Hippocrates (c. 460-377 BC) recommended that men eat lentils, and Aristotle (384-322 BC) added that cooked with saffron, lentils were an unsurpassed aphrodisiac. Plutarch (46-122 BC) claimed that fasolata (Greek bean soup) was a recipe for an unbreakable libido, and according to other initiates, the artichoke was not just an aphrodisiac, but a proven means of conceiving sons.

In her book "Πολύτιμες Αρχαίες Αφροδισιακή Συνταγές" (Unsurpassed Ancient Recipes for Aphrodisiacs), writer Lena Terkesitou reveals some of the foods of love valued and tested by the ancient Greeks, namely:

• Edible bulbs: the ancient Greeks believed that certain bitter bulbs stimulated passion. The bulbs were prepared in the form of a salad with honey and sesame, which are also considered aphrodisiacs.

• Garlic - since time immemorial garlic has been attributed magical and medicinal properties, and the Greeks also revered it as a food of love. In the age of Homer, the Hellenes ate garlic every day. Today, Greeks do not sit down at the table without skordalia, a paste of cheese, garlic, eggs, honey and olive oil.

• Leek - the ancient Greeks considered it an aphrodisiac, probably because of its phallic shape.

• Mushrooms - you will hardly be surprised that even then truffles were famous as an unrivaled aphrodisiac, sold at a fabulous price.

• Satyrio - a species of wild orchid that Dioscorides (c. 40-90), the ancient founder of pharmacology, cited as an excellent love remedy. Plutarch is of the same opinion, who describes the property of the plant in his work Prescriptions for Health (Υγιεινά Παραγγέλματα).

• Staphylinos - a wild plant that, according to the ancients, increased sexual desire, therefore it was used as a love licorice.

BEER LOVE POTION FROM PRAGUE

Goethe called architecture *frozen music*. Prague is an icy music box full of sweetly melancholic tunes. According to some sources, Goethe called beer "the liquid bread of the monks". Czech beer is the bread, the knife, and the crumb. I don't know what Goethe said about crumbs, but in Prague, crumbs are fine. Take, for example, the famous Prague "pečené vepřové koleno" which is pork knee, roasted with horseradish and mustard, with a garnish of pickled hot peppers and an unlimited number of pints of beer.

So, imagine that you have taken your favorite image (that is, yourself) to the fairy-tale Prague, the perfect mise-en-scene for seduction, rapprochement, enjoyment and pacification, you have exhausted yourself from walking around the Old Town and Old Town Squares, you have set your biological clock on Astronomical, you've had your picture taken in front of Jan Hus's monument, you've walked across the Charles Bridge, where you've spat on a saint and whispered a wish to him that will inevitably come true (so beware, more tears are shed over answered prayers, as Saint Teresa says) avoiding the voluptuous Saint Roch, with a jewel just bitten by an evil dog, as well as the Angel of Death (a stinger any way you look at it) and you've climbed up to the medieval castle of Prague Castle. I'm not ruling out the possibility that you picked up half a dozen crystal glasses, some garnet jewelry, and wooden puppets along the way. You'll regret later that you didn't just invest in beer. Better memories remain from that.

Introduction

And at that moment, a cozy beer hall greets you, with terraces and benches, and a Gothic inscription on a wooden sign Na Slamniku (on Wolkerova Street). If you want to believe it, however, beer has been poured here continuously since 1570. At one time, this was the pub of tailors, who often slept on straws (hence the name), probably exhausted from heated trade union activity, and today it is a favorite place for students, cyclists and tourists who were lucky enough to discover the oldest pub in Prague by chance. Only U Kalicha (Na bojišti Street 12-14), immortalized in "The Adventures of the Good Soldier Švejk," can match it.

You settle in and smile sweetly at the waiter. Now you have to say the magic words: "Dám si jedno pivo prosím." This is the Czech equivalent of "Sesame, open up." The waiter immediately breaks into a sweet smile, materializes a mug of frothy copper-amber ambrosia, and hands you a thick notebook. You deploy it. In itself, the reading of the menu strengthens the belief in the coming day. First, because the English translation is the work of the innkeeper's son, a fourth-grader with a wicked sense of humor, and second, because the similarities and differences between the languages of the South Slavic and West Slavic language groups are a recipe for comical misunderstandings and laughter.

The plot gets tangled up

On the first page, a painted duck is wise, subtly hinting to the visitor that the main specialty here is the feathered (aren't they caught straight from the lake in the park?).

The second page is entitled "Proti velque Žízeni" (Against great thirst and hunger), that is beer appetizers. The pub's specialty is Utopenci, you know drowned people. The name is unnatural, but practical, because utopenki turn out to be homemade sausages marinated in vinegar, oil, finely chopped onion, red pepper and a handful of secret spices. There's also Grilované Klobásy, with a warning from the good guy that they're addictive.

Below, a grinning man advises: "For vegetarians." And the excesses begin. Fried ermine (Smažený hermelín). You shudder as you imagine the dainty animal from Leonardo da Vinci's painting smeared drunk (or drunk?!?), but in the next line the fourth-grader graciously explains that it's breaded soft cheese, marinated (nakládaný) or natural. Duh, he got away with it.

It's time for a simple and seemingly innocent delicacy, crispy toasted slices served with a clove of garlic, which you rub on them just before you bite (Topinky s křupavou slaninou a česnekem.). You will be left with sweet memories and bitter regrets when you realize that before being thrown on the grill, they were spread with a thick layer of lard and bacon.

Page three is startlingly blank, with a lone vegetarian dish beneath which eerie Gothic cursive letters proclaim: "The only dish on the menu that never had a mother." The thought of the ill-fated orphan brings tears to your eyes.

And just when you think you've already hardened and hardened and nothing, but nothing can move you, your attention is drawn to the events at the next table. Two youths, adolescent pales in the most literal sense, enter solemnly into the bosom of manhood. That is, they get drunk selflessly and heroically. The waiter, a sly guy with the look of a retired electrician, assisted them with the seriousness of a naturalist. Two equal rows of empty mugs are built on the table, and from the different appearance of the glasses, it can be guessed that the boys have tried all the nuances, filtrations and fermentations of the beer.

Now comes the real challenge. The waiter brings out several bottles of multi-colored liqueurs, becherovkas, and pear schnapps, and sets about pouring them shots. At first they alternate cup - mug, cup - mug, then the game gets rougher and turns into "the cup in the mug and the ex"... Well, please, we can't watch such things.

The menu is far more life-affirming entertainment. Next come the soups, that is, Polévky. Sauerkraut soup is called Zelňačka, garlic is quite predictably called garlic (Česnečka), and onion is not so predictably called cibulačka (Cibulačka). However, the most iconic are the goulash soup (Gulášová polévka) and the beer soup (Pivní polévka), which are served in hollowed-out loaf of bread.

Regarding the "pork", the Czechs with a twinkle in their eye recommend the "Knee!" (Pečené vepřové koleno), a tasty shank with horseradish and mustard, an ambitious project for a single person... Moravian sparrow (Moravský vrabec), which is a call sign for roasted pieces of tender pork, is not to be thrown away either. Tourists are invariably offered Vepřo-knedlo-zelo, which is nice if you like a side of sticky dumplings and not particularly sour cabbage.

As in a masterfully written mystery, the killer appears at the end... The ants are neutralized and the main character in the pub appears on the scene, described generously in two full pages under the title Pivo. The fourth-grader helpfully cited a statistic that the Czechs drink the most beer per capita in the world. He's got it! You immerse yourself in the glories of the famous brands (Pilsner Urquell, Budweisser Budejovicky Budvar, Krusovice, Gambrinus and Staropramen) dark and light, strong and light, pasteurized and unpasteurized (try Bernard), bottled and draft, and the mutterings of "Hallelujah!". Next is the iconic Kozel (meaning goat, of course), which in 2008 won the prestigious Research Institute of Brewing & Malting award for best Czech beer.

The innkeeper's studious son did not fail to note that this May (May 16 - June 1, 2013) Prague will host a world beer festival for the sixth time, a replica of Munich's Oktoberfest, with the promise of huge marquees of goodies and entertainment, where waiters in national costumes will serve 70 Czech beer brands in glass jugs. Hey, after the third pint, you already love that kid!

Not a finale, but a denouement

Any comment is redundant here. The names speak. Horka laska - a dessert with the passionate name "hot love", a combination of creamy ice cream poured with hot raspberry syrup. Although puzzling, the formula Zmrzlinové palačinky s horký malinami a šlehačkou means sweet pancakes with ice cream and raspberry sauce topped with a cap of whipped cream. Sold from tiny shops in the old Czech town of Oplatky, hot thin wafers filled with freshly roasted almonds and chestnuts, as well as the famous Trdlo, are incomparable. Glupak - this is the name of the national delicacy of the Czechs, an emanation of their self-deprecating sense of humor. It is made from vanilla dough rolled on a red-hot metal tube and baked until golden. The finished fool is rolled in crushed almonds and sprinkled with granulated sugar. Why is it called a fool? Well, because it's bloated and hollow, you lap up something, swallow nothing.

Epilogue

The time has come to boldly shout Zaplatítime! You walk blissfully exhausted along the winding streets past basilicas, pointed Gothic towers and art nouveau facades, past the shadows of Franz Kafka and Jaroslav Hasek, of Dvořák and Václav Havel, inhaling the air that inspired Mozart to complete his wonderful opera Don Giovanni, and wink mischievously at Schweik. Na shledanou, Praha!

NEW ORLEANS: GUMBO, JAZZ AND JAMBALAYA

THERE'S NO BETTER TIME to be in New Orleans than Mardi Gras, or Fat Tuesday, the day before Ash Wednesday, which ushers in the 46 days of Catholic fasting before Easter. The streets are filled with a non-stop, lavish and temperamental carnival unlike any other in the world, starting with the perfectly coordinated madness, the jazz, the half-naked mulatto women of Bourbon Street, the combination of French, Creole and Haitian flavor and the fact that the participants in the processions, mounted on moving platforms, throw coins, small sweets and all kinds of gifts into the crowd. The luckiest person is the one who manages to catch a shiny high-heeled slipper. From the neat bakeries wafts the divine fragrance of a tricolor cinnamon bun, known as the "Sladkiš of the three kings" (the three wise men). At the heart of the fluffy treat is a tiny figure of baby Jesus. Whoever lands the figure will host next year's carnival feast.

For a culinary point of view, New Orleans is divided by an invisible line of demarcation between Cajun and Creole culinary traditions.

Cajun cuisine is a mixture of different cultures, traditions and products, a kind of culinary Dixieland that has translated the experiences and tastes of three continents. And like jazz, its main function is improvisation. The roots of this tradition must be sought in the Seven Years' War, which England and France waged on the periphery of the New World in the middle of the 18th century. The Cajuns were French emigrants from Canada who settled in what was then French Louisiana, across the swamplands of the south, leading a life of poverty that earned them the scorn of the rich Creoles. Culturally, they are the originators of the Cajun style of music, incorporating a heritage of French, Native American, African, and Celtic traditions, and of the quirky Cajun cuisine, famous the world over for such delicacies as jambalaya and gumbo.

Gumbo is a spicy thick soup or stew that contains okra, rice, shrimp, poultry, smoked sausage and roux, a sauce of toasted flour and butter, which is constantly whisked in a deep, necessarily cast-iron pan. Another feature is that the ingredients (base, roux, broth, meat, etc.) are cooked separately, then mixed and allowed to simmer together. Classic thickeners are okra or powdered leaves of the American bay tree (fillet). Locals joke that the "Holy Trinity" of their cuisine is celery, green pepper and onion.

Although better known, perhaps because of the melodious chorus-like name that, once in the mouth, stubbornly refuses to leave the mind and heart, jambalaya isn't really that different from gumbo except for the dominant presence of rice and its thickness. A far more exciting culinary challenge is bisque. It is a thick soup, usually made from clams. The dish is typical of southern French, Catalan and Corsican cuisine, being prepared from seafood - mussels, lobsters, crabs and prawns, cooked in a mixture of butter and vegetables with dry white wine and nine spices (onions, leeks, celery, thyme, oregano, bay leaf, basil, black pepper).

Creole cuisine is a completely different story, aristocratic, refined and not so popular. In terms of sweets, however, it is second to none. During the summer months, the famous Creole confectioners prepare hundreds of sotelties, sugar and chocolate sculptures in a variety of wonderful shapes. In the shop windows you can see baskets woven from cotton candy and filled with crystallized sugar flowers, life-sized chocolate mice gnawing on chunks of real cheese and miniature colorful marzipan hummingbirds circling over toasted coconut nests. Coffee and hot chocolate with beaten egg, nutmeg and almonds are also not to be missed.

And in the evening... after midnight, the natives with their rare Creole blood go out into the streets of the French Quarter to sneak into their favorite traps, where the air conditioning is the last concern, but the music is pure magic, and the bottles seem stuck in ice. Locals know that the combination of a decent jazz quartet and a cold beer can make up for almost any adversity. Down from central Bourbon Street are dozens of winding alleys with a vicious reputation (hallelujah!). The humid night hugs you and presses you with scents of flowering bougainvillea and Cuban cigars, sending you among cobbled streets, old houses and wrought iron terraces on which gorgeous mulatto women stretch lazily. And real jazz reigns in the bar, with the undisputed birthright.

Be sure to order a "Hurricane": under the divine sounds of jazz, a magician bartender materializes a glass with crushed ice, grenadine, orange and pineapple juice and pours first light rum, then dark, and finally a killer 75-degree "Bacardi."

It is said that the first cocktail in America was created in New Orleans. At the beginning of the 19th century, the Creole apothecary Anonin Peyzho treated his patients with the murderous Sazeran balm and revived half-dead card players after duels with an ill-fated outcome

(I don't know about vampires). In a glass with crushed ice, the apothecary added a tablespoon of brown sugar, a few drops of Peyzho liqueur (that is, a bitter herbal liqueur), liberally added whiskey and finally added three spoons of absinthe. I don't know about you, but just imagining it and starting to roll down my R's...

SPICE-DO

If the appearance of the spices reflected their significance in world history, the vials would be filled with bright, glittering substances—diamonds, rubies, emeralds, and gold. You open the bottle and from inside comes a cloud with a magical color and a mystical aroma that spreads gently in the space. Since the dawn of human civilization, spices have inspired global trade, research expeditions, wars and poems. In different eras, spices were a currency of exchange - the Pharisees in Judea paid tithes with cumin, in 410 the king of the Visigoths Alaric conquered Rome and demanded a ransom including 3000 pounds of black pepper, in 14th century Germany one pound of nutmeg was exchanged for seven well-guarded the ox. The ground black pepper, with which we generously season the dish, was once valued as much as gold, and nutmeg became the cause of a war that ended with the annexation of Long Island to England.

Far, far away...

Spices are mentioned in the Epic of Gilgamesh, the Bhagavad Gita and the Old Testament. Archaeologists have discovered spices in Egyptian tombs dating back to 3000 BC. The strong preservative properties of spices make them the ideal embalming agent. The Egyptians associated most spices with a certain god. The Bible, the Koran and Ethiopian history tell that in the first millennium B.C. The Queen of Sheba visited King Solomon, bringing him gifts of spices, gold and precious stones. In those days, a handful of cardamom was worth a year's wages, and slaves were bought and sold for a few bowls of black pepper. In the famous Ebers papyrus from 1550 BC. surgery and medicine are also discussed. There we find a rich list of medicines based on herbs and spices, some of which we use in the kitchen to this day. Temples burned the famous kifi incense (the name means "greeting to the gods"), which induced hypnotic states, banished anxiety, cured asthma and acted as a universal antidote.

Mesopotamia: circa third millennium BC cuneiform tablets describe the use of herbs and spices in the fertile valleys between the Tigris and Euphrates, mentioning plants such as cardamom, coriander, garlic, thyme, saffron, turmeric, sesame, anise, fennel, and myrtle. The magical religion of Babylon worshiped the moon as the ruler of healing and medicinal plants. That's why the herbs were harvested in the moonlight.

India: spices such as black pepper, cinnamon, turmeric and cardamom grown here have been used for millennia. In the 4th century BC the ancient surgeon Susruta noted that he used white mustard to "drive away evil spirits" from hospital premises and applied a sesame poultice to post-operative wounds. Ayurveda also relies on the healing and antiseptic properties of spices.

Ancient Greece and Rome: Hellenes traded Eastern spices throughout the Mediterranean and added cumin and poppy seeds to bread, fennel to vinegar, coriander to meat and wine, mint to meat sauces. Garlic is a favorite spice of the commoners, and revelers wear wreaths of parsley and oregano to ward off drunkenness. One word, arómata, means incense, perfume, spices, and aromatic medicines. The legendary magaleion incense, prepared by a perfumer named Megalus from resin, cassia, cinnamon and myrrh, was used to treat wounds and inflammations. Hippocrates, the "father of botany" Theophrastus and Dioscorides described and applied the properties of hundreds of spices and plants.

In the early Roman Empire, exotic spices came mainly from Ancient Arabia. The Arab merchants who jealously guarded the sources and origin of the sought-after commodity and invented fantastic stories about the dangers involved in extracting the spices. The Romans were quite extravagant in their love of herbs and spices – they generously flavored and seasoned wine, balsamic vinegar, olive oil and other noble bath oils. Spices are used for poultices and healing patches. With the expansion of the Roman Empire from the northern side of the Alps, the Goths, Vandals and Huns, who until then only knew onions, rosemary and thyme, experienced their first encounter with black pepper and Eastern spices.

Europe in the Middle Ages: with the Crusades (1096), international trade flourished. Gradually, the price of Asian spices is falling and they are becoming more affordable. They are used to mask unpleasant tastes and smells, but also because of their healing properties. Drawing on Arabic medical texts, European apothecaries prepared medicines from various plants and spices. Charlemagne (742-814) was the first crowned person to show a governmental interest in the cultivation of spices, obliging farmers to grow anise, fennel, fenugreek, sage, thyme, parsley and coriander. In 1180, King Henry II founded the Pepper Merchants' Guild, the forerunner of today's greengrocers. The guild managed the trade in spices, including their purification and storage. But in addition to healing, embalming and beautifying, spices play a crucial role in the exploration of our planet. It is as if the dissatisfaction with the familiar green spices in the garden drives people to explore the unknown territories.

The Great Geographical Discoveries: In the 13th and 14th centuries, Italy monopolized trade with the Middle and Far East. Guilds of grocers, spice merchants, apothecaries, perfumers, and glovers controlled the importation of vast quantities of spices used to disinfect cities against plague and other diseases. The purpose of Marco Polo's journey to China was to bypass the Arab middlemen and convince the Asians to trade directly with Genoa. When Christopher Columbus set foot on the shores of the New World, he intended to make Spain a leading power in the spice trade. Tobacco, coca leaves, vanilla, potatoes and chili brought from North and South America are of great interest to the rest of the world. Meanwhile, the Portuguese discovered the sea route to India, bypassing the southernmost point of Africa ("Cape of Storms", later renamed "Cape of Good Hope"). In 1498 Vasco da Gama's sailors exclaimed, "Christos e espiciarias!" ("For

Christ and spices!"). The Golden Age in the spice trade is coming. True, the journeys hold great dangers, but the payoff often takes rare and beautiful forms—gold, silver, ivory, ebony, spices, exotic animals, and unseen plants. Here we must remind that despite their exotic flavors and aromas, which undoubtedly opened the door to new culinary worlds, until then spices were mainly used as medicines. Even in 1602, when the Dutch-Portuguese Spice War broke out, and later the Dutch-English War, one of the most sought-after spices turned out to be nutmeg. At the same time, not because the queen is addicted to desserts with this spice, but because nutmeg was considered a miracle cure against the plague that was raging in London, which in 1603 sent more than 35,000 people to the grave. No matter the place or era, a number of spices were celebrated as aphrodisiacs. The famous English botanist Culpeper prescribed ginger to his "weak in the affairs of Venus" patients. When Hernán Cortés discovered vanilla in Mexico and brought it to Europe, a German doctor conducted extensive long-term research and scientifically proved that vanilla cures male impotence.

The New World: In the late 17th century, North America also became involved in the spice trade. Boston-born Elihu Yale grew up in England, where he worked as a clerk for the British East India Company, which held a monopoly on all trade with India. Company ships brought the first shipments of nutmeg and cloves from the Moluccas, also known in the Middle Ages as the Spice Islands, to Indonesia. Yale rose to become governor of Madras, and the spice fortune contributed to the establishment of Yale University.

How about today?

Today, spices are everywhere, and at a fairly affordable price. Who can imagine life without the aromatic leaves, seeds, barks and grains for which wars were once fought and expeditions undertaken? Still, the next time you reach for the pepper grinder or the vanilla, remember the advice of the Mistress of Spices - ginger and mango restore love and family, turmeric washes away anger and pain, lotus root attracts new love and fulfills dreams, vanilla repels fears, and the nutmeg in the pocket is the gambler's secret amulet.

FRAGRANCES BY THE BLUE DANUBE

Vienna is the only world capital that has become the godmother of its own culinary style, Viennese cuisine. With aristocratic moderation, she drew inspiration from the culinary traditions of dozens of cultures that touched her imperial splendor to create a thrilling gastronomic poetry. In addition, the 700 hectares of Viennese vineyards leave a unique imprint on the appearance of the city and the winemaking tradition of the region.

For us Bulgarians, Vienna is the closest and most understandable Western European capital. Relations between Bulgaria and Austria date back to the Middle Ages and the early modern era. Until the Liberation, these relations were conditioned by the long conflict between the Habsburg Monarchy and the Ottoman Empire, which, however, did not exclude commercial ties and cultural influences.

Good morning, Vienna

You go out for a brisk morning walk. Strolling down Kärtnerstrasse past fancy shop windows and elegant frizzy old ladies walking poodles, Yorkshire terriers and other pocket sized puppies in something between baby and shopping carts. Time for the first cup of coffee. You slip into a charming corner cafe. There are two possibilities – to order a classic Viennese melange or to get lost among the mysterious signatures on the menu. Only the defunct Pocket Coffee Guide can help you navigate Melange - espresso with frothed milk, Verlängerter - espresso served with hot water, Kapuziner - small mocha with chantilly cream, Franziskaner - melange with chantilly cream, Schwarzer – short black coffee, Kleiner Brauner – small black coffee with cream and Kaffee Verkehrt – coffee with milk.

The mythology of the triumphal coffee procession is associated with the second Ottoman siege of the Austrian capital (July 14 – September 12, 1683). The chronicles describe the rout of the hundred thousand army of the ominous Kara Mustafa thanks to the timely intervention of the Polish troops. The invaders left behind countless provisions, including dozens of sacks of coffee, which the Viennese mistook for fodder. According to some sources, they captured a small Moorish slave who prepared the invigorating drink before their eyes. The black boy with a red fez is immortalized on the packaging of the famous Austrian coffee "Julius Meinl". According to others, the Polish spy Georg Franz Kolszycki, who was in the Kaiser's service and played an important role in the hostilities, demanded the abandoned coffee sacks as a reward. He opened the first Viennese cafe "Under the Blue Bottle" (Zur Blauen Flasche) near St. Stephen's Cathedral. And because the customers were not charmed by the unfamiliar taste, Kolszycki began to strain the strong brew and refine it with milk and sugar, creating the first Viennese melange.

On 10 November 2011, UNESCO listed Viennese coffeehouses as Intangible World Heritage, described as places where "you enjoy the time and the space, but only the coffee is on the bill". So don't miss out on celebrating life at the Wiener Kaffeehaus, a true institution in the Austrian capital.

"You watch couples hovering over a cup of coffee for hours, every day for ten years. Nice marriage, you think. No. The coffee is good."

Alfred Polgar, Viennese writer and journalist, regular visitor to Cafe Central

But coffee is sad without apple strudel, kaiserschmaren or a piece of chocolate history

You can't go wrong with an airy imperial omelet (Kaiserschmarren). Franz Joseph's favorite breakfast is a fluffy fantasy of milk, sugar, eggs and raisins. Another classic treat is apple strudel. For several years, demonstrations of the preparation of Viennese apple strudel have been held at the Residenz Café bakery in Schönbrunn Palace (Schloss Schönbrunn, Kavalierstrakt 52). As a bonus, viewers get the original recipe to make the treat at home.

And for chocolate connoisseurs, Vienna keeps a magical creation... The famous "Sacher" cake appeared in the world in 1832, when the all-powerful Prince Clemens von Metternich (his catchphrase is that the Balkans start from Renweg, i.e. from Vienna) ordered his high-ranking guests to be surprised with a divine dessert. "Try not to embarrass me tonight," he warns the servants. But on that particular day, the chef is not in the palace! They assign the highest order to 16-year-old Franz Sacher, a second degree apprentice. The debut of the young confectioner, a soft fluffy chocolate cake with an ethereal layer of apricot jam under the chocolate glaze, was a huge success. His talent did not go unnoticed and Franz completed his studies in the palaces of Prince Esterházy in Bratislava and Budapest. Already an accomplished chef, Franz began working for himself, betting on his ingenious creation. Soon the "Sacher cake" became the most famous Viennese pastry.

In 1998, master confectioners at the Sacher Vienna Hotel made an original Sacher cake with a diameter of 2.5 meters, and thus the treat entered the Guinness Book of Records.

Supported and with your senses awakened, you can immerse yourself in the beauties of Vienna. The opera house, the Schonbrunn Palace, the Belvedere Palace with its beautiful gardens and a fantastic collection of Gustav Klimt paintings, St. Stephen's Cathedral, the Spanish Riding School, the nostalgic tram No. 1 that makes a complete circuit of the center along the ring-shaped Ringstrasse, the romantic carriage ride of graceful horses or go shopping in the Bermuda Triangle between Kertnerstrasse, Graben and the Hofburg Palace, where you can find a series of second-hand shops, with unique creations by Dior, Chanel, Vivienne Westwood and Gucci, at affordable prices... Whatever you choose, whatever you do, one thing is certain...

It's almost time for lunch

Several delicious options open up to you. If you want to satisfy your hunger quickly, don't miss the small stalls for Wiener Würstel. The master tosses them on the grill to sizzle and get an appetizing tan before brushing them with mustard and tucking them into a lightly toasted bun. Sausages are a favorite delicacy of the Viennese, regardless of class or origin. The Bitzinger stalls are said to be the tastiest, offering wursts, hotdogs and Guerreiner (cheese sausage) with various toppings, as well as draft wine.

If you are an artistic soul, you can take a break in the concert hall's service cafeteria (Am Konzerthaus) – just tell the doorman that you are going to the cafeteria. You grab an alaminute, a sandwich, a pretzel, fruit, a glass of Riesling or a draft beer, sit at a table and immerse yourself in the warm waters of Viennese bohemia. From time to time, a hoarse voice calls out from the intercom, calling actors, directors and stagehands to rehearsal... Watch out, it's no wonder you are also called to play the part of Ophelia, Hamlet or Lady Macbeth...

If you are near the Belvedere, you can go down through the park, exit onto Rennweg and immediately turn right. You will find yourself in front of one of Vienna's most popular pubs, Salm Brau. A great place with a huge copper cauldron in the middle of cozy wooden tables and benches, several types of live Austrian beer, huge portions of pork knuckle and beer soup. If you go between 3pm and 5pm, you'll hit Happy Hour when everything is half price, including giant pints of beer! Above the bar hang certificates and awards for the best Viennese schnitzel in several consecutive years, as well as a copy of the opinion of the Austrian Foreign Ministry from 1970: "Vienna schnitzel can be prepared according to tradition and according to the expectations of consumers only from veal" (Frankfurter Allgemeine Zeitung 19.08.1970). Other subtleties are the size (the schnitzel should protrude slightly from the plate), the breading (it should be as loose as a jogging suit, not as tight as a diving suit), and the garnish of lemon wedges, greens and potato salad.

And if you still have the energy to think about dinner...don't miss the heuriger

THE WORD "HEURIGER" means not only an inn, but also young wine, which is considered such until November 11 (Saint Martin's Day). In a pleasant atmosphere, you will taste the wonderful Viennese wines, white and slightly carbonated, with fruity fresh notes and a festive spirit.

A Piece of Advice:

Buy your Vienna Card. It costs only €18.50 and is valid for 72 hours, giving you a discount on all tickets for museums, public transport, restaurants and shops.

ZURICH: 12 FLAVORS IN 12 HOURS

What a wonderful reputation - aristocracy and opulence, order and safety, modern art and delicious delights. No, it's not a dream, it's Zurich!

You wake up and look out the window - Lake Zurich against the background of the Alps... You review the pre-marked program, distributed and organized with the precision of a Swiss watch, take the permanent arsenal (guidebook, camera, raincoat, sunglasses) and boldly move forward!

8.45 am

You find yourself on Bahnhofstrasse, the most expensive street in Europe, embodying the financial might of Switzerland and Zurich, just in time for breakfast. Here, the working day begins at eight o'clock, and an hour later there is a fifteen-minute break for breakfast ("tsnyuni"). Cafes, gardens and city benches are filled with elegant clerks who eat croissants, buns and the local classics, muesli with yogurt or grated apple, which at the beginning of the last century the Swiss doctor Bircher-Benner proclaimed to be the most nutritious breakfast. You pop into the nearby boulangerie and grab yourself a crunchy "nusgipfel," generously sprinkled with nuts and a white sugar glaze that would send French croissants into a deep depression. You sit on a high chair next to the window, take a sip of coffee and give warm thanks for the Italian thread in the Swiss tale. Immerse yourself in the discreet glamor of luxury jewelry and watch stores, fashion boutiques of famous designers, banks and hotels, exquisite patisseries and the jingle of trams. Beneath your feet are vaults like Ali Baba's cave, filled with gold, diamonds, and untold riches. Just opposite, on the Paradeplatz, where the guild parade and the city carnival start, is the historic Sprüngli Patisserie (Sprüngli, Bahnhofstrasse 21), which dates back to 1836. From a distance, the windows could easily be mistaken for a jewelry store, filled with perfect pralines, truffles, trademark miniature macaroons (Luxemburgerli) and cakes.

A little further down the street is the cult restaurant Zeughauskeller (Bahnhofstrasse 28a), one of the oldest in Zurich and located in the former armory. The restaurant offers sausages from all cantons and regional cuisines in Switzerland, including the superb specialties Schüblig (raw beef or pork sausage) and Neuchatelois Saucisson (the recipe includes 2/3 pure pork and 1/3 bacon, mixed with pepper, garlic and salt, forming incredible deliciousness, which is served slightly toasted, with a garnish of vegetables). Here, be sure to try some of the amazing Swiss beer (Appenzell Beer, the most popular brands are Quöllfrisch and Vollmond), which is brewed by hand, from fresh ingredients and using traditional methods. But for the merits of Swiss gastronomy later, now it's time for a walk.

Backed up, you take a left towards St Peter's Church, just enough to catch a glimpse of the imposing clock tower and head towards the Lindenhof in the historic heart of Zurich. There was once a Roman castle here, and later a Carolingian palace and the palace of Charlemagne's grandson, Charlemagne. On the square there is a fountain dedicated to the events of 1291, when during the siege of the city by the Austrian Duke Albert I, the women of Zurich went out to fight dressed in military uniforms. There is a fantastic view of the whole city, the Grossmünster church, Lake Zurich and the Alps, and the river Limat. Finally, you enter the Fraumünster Church to view stained glass windows by Marc Chagall and Augusto Giacometti. At one time, the abbess of this nunnery for aristocratic individuals had enormous influence over the fate of the city and even had the privilege of minting coins.

14.45

Either intuitively or following the directions of the guidebook, at noon you find yourself on the Marktgasse. The cobbled streets of the 12th-century old town sparkle with cleanliness, and the blue vintage tram glides by silently like a romantic whiff of the past. Restaurants are already deceiving tourists with a detailed description of the day's menu - the traditional Zürich dish Zürigschnätzlets (small pieces of beef in a cream and wine sauce), which is served with crispy Rösti potato pancakes (those with onions, white wine and cream are the tastiest) or the small Chnöpfli dumplings. You make sure that fondue, raclette and bratwurst continue to be the backbone of the Swiss diet. Starving college kids nibble on grilled bratwurst at a nearby street stall, and petite Japanese women nibble on toasted pretzels. You come across a coffee shop, marvel at the exotic varieties and aromas, and the huge old mill. Across the street is a cafe that serves lovely hot chocolate. You drink a cup of thick ambrosia while reading a brochure on the history of chocolate in Switzerland. The country boasts the highest consumption of chocolate in the world (11.6 kg per capita per year). At the end of the 19th century, Swiss chocolate enjoyed an excellent reputation in Europe, thanks to the creators of milk chocolate, Daniel Peter and Rodolphe Lind. It turns out that the cartographers of chocolate in Europe are Swiss - the Josti brothers conquer Berlin, Salomon Wolff and Tobias Beranger open the famous Café Chinois in St. Petersburg, the Kloetta brothers open factories in Scandinavia, and Carl Faser opens a store in Helsinki. Even Belgian chocolate has Swiss roots, thanks to Jean Neuhaus and his son Frederic, who in 1912 created the first pralines in Brussels...

On the way, you eat a humble pretzel from the neat stall (Brezel König) and enter the Kunsthaus museum, which, luckily for you, is open on Wednesdays for free. In addition to the collection of classical and contemporary fine art with canvases by Salvador Dali, Monet, Picasso and Chagall, as well as works by the Swiss sculptor Alberto Giacometti. You pass the legendary Café Odéon, opened on July 1, 1911, to become a center of attraction for intellectuals and bohemians (suffice it to mention Stefan Zweig, Somerset Maugham, Erich Maria Remarque, James Joyce and Albert Einstein). Next door is another key

Zurich venue, Bellevue, a favorite for concerts and attractions. You end the afternoon at Grossmünster Church, with its adjoining men's monastery, which rivaled the Fraumünster nunnery throughout the Middle Ages.

18.45

It's getting late, you're out of energy, but you have a voracious appetite, so you consider the dozen tempting offers and promotional brochures you've picked up along the way. You can dine in one of the dozens of restaurants on Niederdorfgasse, the most touristic street in Zurich, such as the traditional restaurant Adler Swiss Chuchi. The idea of dining at Blinde Kuh ('Blind Cow'), where the chefs and waiters are blind and the lounge is shrouded in sense-sharpening blackness, is dropped for lack of a reservation.

Finally, you choose the historic restaurant "zum Kropf" (In Gassen 16), a famous place since the Middle Ages. The name of the house was mentioned for the first time in 1444, a private residence until the end of the 19th century and a favorite place of prominent city families. Until 1462, the house belonged to the city armorer, at the end of the 18th century it passed into the hands of the mayor, and in 1881 the wealthy Anna Müller-Flack turned it into an elegant spice shop. The house then became a famous beer hall, and from 1909 it was probably the most famous restaurant in Zurich. The menu offers traditional specialties - crusty bread, raclette (melted cheese served with potatoes, pickles and onions), warmed Älplermagronen (a nutritious dish of potatoes, macaroni, cheese, cream and onions, with a garnish of baked apple) and most finally... the holy grail of Swiss cuisine, the divine appetizing fondue!

"The fondue is for the locals..." the waiter tells you.

"In a country where people eat fondue from a common dish, there can be no war," you reply.

You order, free from remorse about quantities and calories. A short explanatory text on the menu says that fondue appeared in the 18th century as a kind of culinary invention, allowing people to use dried cheeses and stale bread in winter. A clay pot, a few pieces of Emmental, Gruyère or Fribourgois, a few cloves of garlic, a pinch of fragrant alpine spices, a little wine – and the caldera of molten golden lava in which to melt hard bread is ready! You skewer the first piece on the long skewer and scoop up the melted treat and take a sip of the tart wine.

That is the Swiss nirvana.

BRUSSELS: THE COOK'S DELIGHT AND DIVINE BEER

Blessed are the residents of Brussels, the Belgian capital of the European Union, because whoever has not tried the bewitching abundance of beer, the challenging taste and quantity of moules frites, the magical chocolates and waffles that saturate the small streets around Picliot with their fragrance, is blessed to get to know the city with the senses the beginner. Belgian cuisine combines the best of French, German and Dutch culinary traditions. Each area is distinguished by a unique specialty, a kind of appetizing business card.

But let's get our ducks in a row...

Any gastronomic and tourist tour of Brussels starts from the Grand Place (Grand-Place or Grote Markt, according to the Walloon or Flagship version). The exquisite jewel, decorated with Gothic and Baroque buildings, is not accidentally included in the UNESCO World Heritage List. Grand Place is a favorite for locals and tourists alike, especially if you only have a day or two in Brussels. The small streets around offer a fine selection of gourmet delights, souvenir shops, chocolatiers and architectural masterpieces from the era of European commercial prosperity. In the evening, a walk on the Grand Place is a real delight for the senses - elegantly dressed people from all over the world, classy street musicians, artists and performers, performances and improvisations covering the entire spectrum from traditional art to artful provocation. Be sure to stroll through the Galeries Saint-Hubert, which is the oldest covered shopping arcade in Western Europe and dates back to 1847, offering a fine selection of shops, restaurants, cafés, cinemas and theatres. If you have more time, visit Café Bota in the Botanic Garden (Rue Royale 236 Koningsstraat) to enjoy avant-garde bands and parties, taste unforgettable culinary creations of Brussels' top culinary schools and drink divine draft beer, of course. at affordable prices.

Other hidden treasures are the Halles (Halles Saint-Géry at Place Saint-Géry 25/Sint-Goriksplein 25), built on the site of the 16th-century Church of Saint-Géry. There were once four mills in this historic city center, a major source of power in medieval industry. The Halls of Saint-Géry were built in 1881 around an obelisk, a creation of the Belgian architect Dubois.

Today, in addition to the wonderful bistro with draft beer, hot chocolate and delicious dishes, it houses two associations charged with the preservation of the cultural and natural heritage of Brussels, as well as a number of exhibitions, social events and cultural events. Finally, if you like culinary challenges in ultra-modern setting and bohemian company, enter the depths of the cult establishment Belga Queen (Rue du Fosse-aux-Loups 32). We promise you an unforgettable experience.

You will inevitably be entangled in the fragrant webs of Belgian chocolate

BRUSSELS MAY BE KNOWN as the international capital of Europe and host to the administrative offices of the European Union, but foodies know that the city is actually the capital of chocolate.

Passionate fans of the food of the gods can touch the Lord of Haute Couture chocolate and visit Pierre Marcolini's store on the Place du Grand Sablon. The subdued, elegant interior is reminiscent of a sophisticated fashion boutique, and the handmade truffles and chocolates are arranged in minimalist black boxes. A black plush carpeted staircase leads to the second floor, where decadent opulence reigns. What more eloquent explanation of love than the miniature crimson chocolate heart in the center of each candy box, sunk in depths of red and black rustling paper... Another unique Belgian chocolate adventure is the "caraque" (caraque, a large three-masted commercial sailing ship used in the 16 and 17th century), fantastic dark chocolate pralines with Kriek cherry beer, milk chocolate with spéculoos biscuits and white chocolate with pear filling... And if you are not a geek, but just love chocolate, you can choose, taste and applaud the delights of Godiva, Leonidas, Corné Port-Royal, Galler, Cote d'Or, Dolfin or Neuhaus... Whatever you choose, you won't go wrong because the composition of Belgian chocolate is regulated by a law from 1884. It guarantees a minimum level of 35% pure cocoa.

And if you still have room and courage for sweet temptations

Don't miss the Belgian waffles, crispy and golden on the outside and soft and airy on the inside. What sets Belgian waffles apart from all their cousins is their larger size, lighter dough (thanks to added yeast) and a special baking grid that forms deep pockets capable of holding ethereal chocolate sauce, ice cream, fresh strawberries and whipped cream.

In case you are not planning such adventures, you are waiting for...

Beer, in all shades of amber, from the delicately creamy white wheat beer Witbier, traditionally flavored with coriander and orange peel, through all shades of gold to the intoxicating, gorgeous reddish-brown and chocolate tones of ale, with a dense malt presence and delicate fruit flavors. The trademark of Brussels is the aromatic lambic beer, the result of spontaneous fermentation with wild yeasts that thrive only there, and flowing in barrels in which wine was previously aged. It is a cheerful, sparkling, exciting ambrosia that will fill you with inspiration and passion for life.

The next temptation is the seasonal or house ale, with a fruity character and a delicate aftertaste, a lighter version of lambic. Some breweries flavor it with herbs and spices to enhance its flavor. Around Christmas, dozens of small breweries compete to tempt connoisseurs and innocent tourists alike with fantastic flavors and recipes, often dating back to the Middle Ages (which can't have been all that dark to have given birth to just such a beer...).

Trappist beer is produced by or under the control of Trappist monks. Only ten abbeys in the world, six of them in Belgium, produce

Trappist beer and have the right to put the "Authentic Trappist Product" logo on the labels.

Next comes the clan of double-fermented beers, a Flemish dubbel, a full-bodied ale with an amber to brown color and a rich, roasted malt aroma. It intrigues the palate with a hint of spices and fruit.

And finally we come to the triples (strong triple ale), produced according to authentic recipes from the 16th and 17th centuries. Their origin takes us back to the Trappist and abbey breweries, where 300 years ago the monks combined three types of grain - wheat, oats and barley. Usually, these are light beers with a bronze to golden color, light hop bitterness, a harmonious fruity taste of banana and vanilla, and a rich bouquet of aromas with hints of orange and citrus fruits. The recommended serving temperature is 6 - 9 °C.

Subtly, we come to beer's faithful friend, fries

Here, fried potatoes (Frites) occupy a special place, because the Belgians swear that in the distant 14th century it was they who gave the world the delicious temptation. They are prepared in dozens of booths and shops, in cardboard funnels, necessarily with mayonnaise garnish. Moreover, in 2008 in the charming Belgian city of Bruges, a special Museum of French Fries opened its doors.

And if you are still in the mood for tasty adventures, you can complete the gastronomic expedition with moules frites, that is steamed freshly caught mussels with a giant portion of fried potatoes, Anguille au Vert - eel in a green sauce with fresh spices and herbs, Asparagus à la Flamande - Asparagus in a cream sauce, Boudin Blanc & Boudin Noir – white and black blood pudding or Ghent's signature dish, Waterzooi – a thick chicken soup, sometimes with fish.

IMAGINE ... AMSTERDAM

Imagine... imagine that your good friend, like-minded and Dutch colleague offers you an avant-garde for the Balkans and common for Europe adventure called Home Swap, i.e. exchange of housing, lifestyle and philosophy for two weeks. As a result, the Dutch woman, together with the man and their two children, find themselves in a hereditary panel apartment in Mladost, and you and the household migrate temporarily to Amsterdam. And the fun begins...

The hostess, with the inherent Dutch common sense and pragmatism, has left a notebook with invaluable advice and instructions, a kind of Modus operandi for Balkans in Amsterdam. You left her phone at the Emergency...

Day one: check-in in a serene, smiling narrow abode by a canal, in which ducks and swans swim, with baby swans at that. Surprise one - there are no curtains on the windows (and they are large, almost from floor to ceiling). That's why there are orchids. The notebook helpfully informs you that the tradition of bare windows has at least three explanations. The first, as dwellings were heated by live fire fireplaces in those days, midnight fires were a frequent occurrence, and neighbors in opposite buildings could quickly raise the alarm and save householders and property. Explanation two, in a country of sailors and merchants, wives guarded their good name in the absence of their husbands by showing that there was nothing and no one to hide behind the lowered curtains. Explanation three, the majority of Dutch people are Protestant. They lived in parishes where everyone knew everyone else. And the good tone demanded that the good Christian should not hide his life behind thick curtains, which inevitably suggested sin... What's more, those who still dared to put up curtains paid a penalty fee.

You unfold the Book of Wisdom and begin to read aloud the precious instructions:

"Dear guests, welcome to our flat country with a rich history as a dominant economic power in Europe. Land of great thinkers such as Hugo de Groot, the father of international law and Wilhelm of Orange Count of Nassau, leader of the Dutch revolt against the Spanish, of artists such as Vincent van Gogh, Rembrandt Harmenson van Rijn and scientists. You're in luck because you're in the heart of Amsterdam, surrounded by 17th-century ring canals, diamond shops, breweries and distilleries, a city with a laid-back cosmopolitan culture. Our house is small, but has a wonderful view and a central location. The bikes are waiting for you in the parking lot at the end of the street. Ride in the red lane and don't worry about the rules, in an accident the cyclist always has the right. Pedestrians on the cycle lane are fined regardless of the circumstances.

The kitchen is microscopic, so we usually eat out or order takeout. You can have breakfast at the bistro on the corner without paying, there is an account opened in my name. Get yourself a uitsmijter serving with two utensils (we appreciate thrifty people) - includes three fried eggs, bread, cheese and bacon. For children, we recommend Poffertjes – small fluffy pancakes with buckwheat flour, sprinkled with butter and powdered sugar, but for luxury you can choose a topping of caramel syrup (stroop), whipped cream (slagroom) or strawberries (aardbeien)."

Day two: a boat ride on the canals, getting to know the neighbors on the left and right, long handshakes, exchanging names, business cards, courtesies, they invite you for a glass of wine and herring on Friday at exactly 7 p.m., they say "no gifts" and that fills you with serious suspicions that you might expose yourself... But the Book contains a special section on good manners, well done to the housewife.

"The neighbors will surely invite you over." Be sure to bring them some small gift - flowers (they are cheap here), a bottle of wine, a cake or a souvenir from your country. Always greet people by name. Exchanging three kisses on the cheeks is good manners, but remember:

men do NOT kiss men. Be punctual, never be late. If someone stops by our house, treat them to coffee with milk and sugar. And caramel waffles (stroopwafel). It is a Dutch delicacy first prepared in the town of Gouda in the distant 18th century. In fact, until 1870, stroopwafels were only made in Gouda, where there were almost a hundred bakeries specializing in making them. They are served over a cup of coffee so that they swell from the steam and develop their flavor."

Day three: Museum Day. Total exhaustion after a tour of the Royal Museum (Rijksmuseum) with a collection of works by Dutch masters, going wild in front of Rembrandt's Night Shift (1642) and Vermeer's Maid (1658). Next is the Van Gogh Museum, wandering among 200 paintings, 500 drawings and 700 letters, contemplating Peasants Eating Potatoes (1885) and feeling a ferocious hunger worthy of sea wolves...

You go out into the street at dusk, find yourself in the middle of a windy "summer" day and fix a cozy bistro on the corner. You slide in and open the Book, the Something to Eat section.

"All cafes and bars serve Bitterballen - fried balls filled with finely chopped beef, flour, butter, greens and spicy spices, in a crispy breading. They are served with lots of mustard. A perfect appetizer for beer. But if you are very hungry, order a stamppot – a sample of Dutch cuisine. A folk, tasty and nutritious dish that can in no way be called gourmet. It's a few baked and roughly mashed potatoes with a lot of butter and a side of kale, onions and carrots, plus a huge piece of smoked sausage (rookworst).

Day four: sour muscles from relentless pedaling has become your modus vivendi. You're trying to get used to the sweet-salty taste of black licorice candy or just Drop, and you're making hellish plans on how you're going to bring whole bags of this mind-blowing treat to friends, co-workers, and relatives. "How do you eat them?", you ask every Dutch person you meet in bewilderment. "We get used to it from an early age, and when we grow up, we're already hooked and even like them..." You spend the day at the NEMO museum, the largest science museum in the Netherlands, built according to a project by Renzo Piano. A true paradise for children and home-grown experimenters, where thousands of exhibits, appliances and devices offer visitors to try out how they work. Lectures, exhibitions and presentations are held in the adjacent NEMO theater. And in the late afternoon you find another "your" place and open the Book.

"Today is the time to try the Dutch powerhouse Snert or Erwtensoep, a pea soup with sausage, bacon cubes, pork chops and bread, which should be so thick that a spoon can stand upright in it... If you're craving something sweet, get si fruit flan (Limburgse vlaai), a pastry with a crispy crust and a filling of apples, plums, cherries or apricots. Typical of the southern region of Limburg, the pastry originated in the town of Weert, where a certain Maria Hubertina Hendrix used to sell the freshly baked pie on the station platform.

Day six: guests with herring...

After an educational day at the Anne Frank Museum, the time comes for the long-awaited visit to the neighbors on the right. A tall, gaunt violinist and a fine woman with fiery red hair and a freckled round face, with five children between the ages of three and thirteen, two of them adopted. Their home, furnished in white, pale gray and sepia, impresses with a light, soulful, playful interior. After a glass of wine on foot, you are directed to the table where the most famous Dutch specialty awaits you ... fresh, crisp, not to mention almost alive. Hollandse nieuwe haring or in other words, herring. The choice is whether to place the fish on a bun cut lengthwise, with a garnish of chopped onions or pickles, or drop it bare by catching it by the tail and deftly tossing it into your mouth with the head thrown back. Fortunately, the head of the herring has been removed, otherwise one would feel like an anaconda looking its victim in the eye as it devours it. The hosts kindly explain that only the herring caught between May and June is called Hollandse nieuwe. It is prepared according to the Dutch tradition, namely that the freshly caught fish is gutted on board the boat, but the pancreas is left in the belly. Enzymes preserve the herring, which is lightly salted. Does the taste...um, suffocating intense seems to be the most accurate description. Good thing the hostess pours rescue shots of Dutch juniper gin, Jenever. Created in the Netherlands in the 18th century by the doctor Francisco Silvius, who one fine day soaked juniper berries, cumin, anise and some other herbs in alcohol, creating a unique drink originally conceived as a medicine for stomachaches, gallstones and kidney diseases.

The next few days slip away into tulip expeditions, day trips to Utrecht and Rotterdam, a visit to a windmill, and finally, hallelujah, a holiday at a country farm, where you eat Dutch cheese on your stomach and stomp with wooden clogs, in the company of children, tame cows, horses and chickens.

Finally, you come home exhausted and find your home vibrating with cleanliness, tidy and eager to meet its owners.

LA BELLA ITALIA

The life philosophy of the Italians is crystallized in the expression il culto de benessere: to keep the best for yourself, combining the healthy stomach of the peasant with the refined palate of the cardinal. And drinking wine is a whole art that aims to make food and conversation even more enjoyable. And since each area of Botsza is proud of its local specialties, as distinctive and unique as the people who inhabit it, let's take a disarmingly delicious tour of la bella Italia. If you are on an excursion to these places, focus on the local specialties in order to enrich both your taste perceptions and your gastronomic culture.

Rome and the fifth quarter

They say that the real heart of Rome is the old butcher's district of Testaccio. For centuries, countless animals were brought here to be slaughtered, the good meat going to the tables of the nobles and cardinals in the Vatican. The common people had to be content with what remained - the so-called quinto quarto, the "fifth quarter" of the animal: entrails, head, legs and tail. From this sprang a small guild of cooks specializing in the preparation of this "waste." The culinary ingenuity of the Romans was so great that soon even cardinals and nobles were willingly eating dishes such as coda alla vaccinara, oxtail stewed in tomato sauce, and caratella d'abbaccio - heart, lung and spleen of a newborn lamb stewed with onions and white wine If you find yourself in Rome, be sure to try these dishes in one of the local trattorias - what more authentic way to taste this thick, dark, a saturated, bloody city with all its bitter history? The common Roman, connoisseur of dolce vita, loves his food so passionately that no matter how rich he is, he is unlikely to ever step foot into one of the Eternal City's many Michelin-starred restaurants.

Tuscany and virginity... are we talking about olive oil?

IF YOU'RE LUCKY ENOUGH to know Italian, don't be surprised if you hear something like this in Tuscany: "Lucia wants to be a virgin when we get married, like her mother. That's why we had to stop having sex until the engagement." Such an apparently illogical statement does not cause any astonishment among Italians. In a country where fanatically zealous Catholicism is only a generation behind, everyone knows at least as many degrees of virginity in a virgin as there are in olive oil. And it is divided into extra-virgin (first cold pressing), extra-fine virgin (second pressing), extra-fine virgin, and so on down to another dozen and more degrees of virginity and near-virginity, before finally reaching such indescribable depravity that it is simply named "clean" and therefore suitable only for export and for pouring into the lamp.

Naples and Margarita

ACCORDING TO ONE STORY, in 1889 Margherita of Savoy, wife of the Italian King Umberto I, was vacationing at the Caposimonte summer residence near Naples and wanted to try pizza, the food of the Neapolitan poor. And since the court chef had never gotten his hands dirty with such ersatz, they called Raffaello Esposito, owner of the best pizzeria in town. He served Her Majesty three pizzas, two traditional and one improvised in honor of the occasion. Raffaello garnished it with red tomatoes, basil and mozzarella, the colors of the Italian flag. Won't you, the queen liked this particular pizza, and the enterprising Italian immediately named his creation "Margherita". Neapolitans claim that their city is the cradle of fast food with pizzas, donuts or even a roast pig - right on the street.

Torino and espresso

YOU MUST HAVE HEARD all kinds of myths and legends about the divine Italian espresso - soft and tasty, strong and aromatic, covered with cream. Nowhere else in the world can coffee compare to this masterpiece of cafe art. What is the secret? Well, first, the machine. The real Italian barista (cafeteria) recognizes only one brand - the big shiny Gagia – the Harley Davidson of coffee machines. Second, the short Italian espresso, which is pure adrenaline, is only part of the emotion. Because real Italians drink ristretto. A ristretto is made with the same amount of ground coffee as a normal espresso, but with half the water. Its unique taste does not tolerate sugar, just a sip of mineral water and a miniature cornetto croissant sprinkled with powdered sugar. And don't forget: every Italian knows that drinking coffee sitting at a table is bad for digestion, which is why it is penalized with three times the price of drinking it at the bar!

Sicily and desserts

ONCE AN ARAB EMIRATE and later the capital of a Norman kingdom, Palermo was the exotic pearl of Europe. Here, the cuisine and architecture are a magical tangle of Arab-Norman influences with a Byzantine twist. So it is with the cuisine - anchovies, citrus, olives, capers, mint, saffron, chili, garlic, wine and honey combine with the gifts of the land and the sea, giving birth to unimaginable opulence. Desserts are an indescribable creation of the culinary finesse of the Arabs and the rapturous dexterity of the nuns - pastes, curabies, marzipan delights, candied fruits, sherbets and fruit ice creams. Let's not forget the world-famous Marsala sweet wine. Which will remind you of a deeply philosophical Italian proverb: Anni, amori e bicchieri di vino, non se contano mai - Years, lovers and glasses of wine should not be counted.

PARIS - FRENCH FOR BEGINNERS

The French are famous for enjoying life's small (and big!) pleasures, from food and wine to fashion, love and art. In everyday life, this sense of the world is reflected in the coffee culture that flows along the chic boulevards and narrow streets. Coffee has long since become a kind of ritual - it is usually drunk in an open-air cafe, so that you contemplate the eternal river of life, chat with friends or flirt with passers-by.

Eating is another matter. The confusion begins as soon as you cross the threshold of the welcoming-looking bistro. Instead of inviting you, the waiter raises an eyebrow, surveys you haughtily from head to toe, and blurts out the curse: Avez-vous reserve? (Do you have a reservation?)

Um, yes, dining in a Parisian restaurant is aerobatics, requiring advance planning, attention and discipline. First, restaurants serve food only during the strictly defined hours for lunch and dinner - usually from 12:00 to 14:00 and from 19:30 to 23:00. Loyalty to your bistro is proverbial and explains the meaning of the magic word "reservation". Second, here it is normal to wait to be served. You sit for about 15 minutes, and the waiter is nowhere to be found. Well, you have no choice but to shrug your shoulders like a true Frenchman. The explanation? In France, hiring staff is a murderously expensive pleasure, so as a rule, waiters are few in number and terribly overworked. So don't worry - you're in for a long stay anyway (2-3 hours with an aperitif, three courses and coffee and/or digestif after dessert). In France, personal charm is a great power, so a practiced smile can do wonders! Seduction in the French sense of the word - that is, the ability to charm another - is the salt of life. Charm is your most powerful weapon. If you don't use it, the taxi driver will charge you more money, the waiter will look down on you, and you will be given the worst hotel room.

As a rule in the restaurant, you have to ask for the bill, because it is considered extremely rude for the waiter to "rush" you to leave after eating. You won't see drunken revelers here - the French appreciate wine for its taste, not its intoxication, and you won't hear loud voices. "They're like eggshells in a soufflé," say the French.

If you want to learn Parisian manners, first, give it casually and don't be "dumb". Always order a minimum of three courses, regardless of whether you're hungry and eat every last bite (portions are small anyway). Melt your bread in the sauce - here it is the Law of God. Eat cheese before or instead of dessert. The round cheeses are cut like a cake. Drink your coffee with milk in the morning and espresso in the afternoon. Give a small tip, but regularly. Smoke anywhere, anytime. And by no means get into an argument about wine with the sommelier - he knows his job, believe me!

Some subtle tastes

A MAIN POINT IN FRENCH cuisine is the small bouquet of spices bouquet garni. The classic version includes bay leaves, parsley, thyme, wrapped in celery stalks and tied with string or placed in a cheesecloth bag. It is used to flavor soups and broths by placing it during cooking and removing it before serving the dish. You will feel this taste on the tip of your palate.

In 1759, English troops besieged the French island of Majorand and the port of Mayon. Food supplies were running low - only oil and eggs remained. Soldiers and officers were so sick of omelets that the French commander-in-chief, Duke Richelieu, ordered a new dish to be invented. And his master chef created ambrosia, which they named mayonnaise in honor of the city! Be sure to try the French mayonnaise to know what this word means.

Some emotional grounds

You can sit for hours in some charming establishment, meditating over a cup of coffee with cream, without even getting a hint that it's time to go.

Try the warm, freshly baked croissants from the corner boulangerie (cockroach shop), where there's always a line because everyone in the neighborhood knows it's the best. And that's in every neighborhood.

To see the markets with the colorful fruits and vegetables arranged in Cheops pyramids, painstakingly wrapped when purchased in multi-colored paper and tied with curled ribbon...

Appreciate the elegant 80-year-old ladies with flawless hair, make-up, high heels and fishnet tights who just give you confidence that life is wonderful.

To try to taste as much as possible from the more than four hundred scented cheeses and the thousands of wines at a price of less than 5 euros a bottle...

RUSSIAN WINTER

Whether from the habitation of this vast country, sometimes wild, harsh and torturous, sometimes royally rich and extravagant, or because of the indescribable tangle of meetings and separations with other peoples, which obviously had a beneficial effect on the genes, the soul and the philosophy of life, the Russians are the only Slavs , which boast the passion of the Latin Americans tempered in the inhuman cold of Siberia, the intellectual sophistication and reading of the old Europeans, the childlike generosity of the Bedouins and the impressive wisdom of the Asians. Can you think of any other nation whose representatives are capable of getting heroically drunk discussing the classics of their literature, getting up at early dawn, purifying themselves inside and out in the authentic bath, rolling in the snow (the men) or passing through the skilled hands of the hairdresser (the women) and to appear tanned and rosy-cheeked in spite of the murderous hangovers of the rest of the non-Russian diners, ready to breakfast with hot tea in glass cups and fantastic black caviar pies...

Caviar

Russians appreciated what a delicacy black caviar is already 300-400 years ago. Originally a "fasting food" replacing meat in the 200-day Orthodox fast, it became a favorite delicacy of aristocrats. Peter the Great displayed an entrepreneurial spirit and had 50 specially trained fishermen on the shores of the Caspian Sea, guaranteeing a constant supply. Hardly finished with the revolution, the strict Bolsheviks declared the production of caviar a state monopoly... as it remains on paper to this day. Russians are convinced that caviar is a healthy, protein-rich ambrosia that energizes sex, improves eyesight and slows down the effects of alcohol. Russian doctors invariably prescribe to patients the "holy trinity" of caviar, mineral water and pomegranates...

The sturgeon, one of the oldest living creatures on the planet, the largest and longest-lived freshwater fish, spawns only between the ages of 8 and 15. Come to think of it, I don't know if she lays eggs or just gold and dollars... She, along with her close relatives - the whiting and trout, spawns only three times in her life. The value of caviar varies according to quality, which is determined by the age-old natural (and why not economic?) law of scarcity, namely, the harder you get something, the more you want it. The largest caviar, called beluga, is the most expensive and is obtained from the largest females. The highest quality beluga is almost unknown outside of Russia, which again reminds us of the distinctive Russian aristocracy.

Osetra is the name of the medium-sized caviar, and the smallest is called sevruga. As for the color, connoisseurs know that true black caviar is not black... On the contrary, the lighter the berry, the more valuable it is. The most desirable should be amber, with a very slight fishy aroma, the grains should be shiny, uniform in size and not stuck together. Caviar is never frozen, so its processing plants are located only on the coast where it is harvested, an expert taster tastes each batch to classify it and determine how much salt to add.

The bad thing is that this delicacy, outward sign of wealth, horse medicine and aphrodisiac will soon enter the red book of endangered species. Terrifying statistics indicate that over the past 15 years the population of sturgeon in the Caspian Sea has decreased 40 times... But let's not be pessimistic - now we are on Russian territory, so we are obliged to honor the most notable ruler of all time, Catherine the Great (1729-1796), who every morning had tea with vodka and an omelette with caviar for breakfast... This German princess, married at a very young age to the Russian heir to the throne, Grand Duke Peter, found a way to get rid of her confused husband. Crowned Empress of Russia, she reigned for half a century with an iron hand in a velvet glove. She spoke four languages, was interested in art and philosophy, had a whole bunch of official lovers led by the tense Potemkin and countless one-night stands. And since the great historical figures dragged their feet, it would be a sin to leave out those immortalized in dozens of novels and movies...

Beef Stroganoff

The history of the famous dish Beef Stroganoff goes back to the end of the 19th century, when the chef of the famous Russian general, Count Pavel Alexandrovich Stroganov (1795-1891), invented the recipe for a culinary competition in St. Petersburg, although the recipes for stewed in sour cream sauce meat, are typical of medieval Russian cuisine. After the fall of the Russian Empire, the dish became popular in Chinese hotels and restaurants before the start of World War II. Russian and Chinese immigrants, as well as American servicemen stationed in pre-communist China, brought several variations of the dish to the US, which probably accounts for its popularity in the 1950s. Russian Beef Stroganoff is usually served with noodles, porridge or, as a last resort, with potatoes.

For generals, shashlik and pelmeni

And since it was about generals, we should mention that the tradition of imperial raids in Central Asia and Siberia in the east and in the Caucasus in the south had a beneficial effect on the Russian culinary essence. The cuisine of the Caucasian dominions (Georgia, Armenia and Azerbaijan) brings a touch of exoticism to the unpretentious Russian table, headed by shashlik (from shashka, meaning saber), made from marinated pieces of meat roasted on a spit. Russian shashlik preserves the Georgian custom of being prepared from beef fillet. The typical marinade is red wine, onion and garlic, pepper and salt. As for the pure form of icy exoticism, it erupts into the Siberian equivalent of Italian tortellini - pelmeni.

The hosts from the frosty North tried to get some benefit out of the nightmarish climate and prepared hundreds of pieces at a time, storing them outside in the natural natural freezer. Today, all over Russia there are benches and stalls for pelmeni, which can be measured in popularity with the American hot dog and Italian pizza by the slice... The dough is simple - flour, water, egg and salt, the filling is usually minced meat with a lot onion. The treat always goes with the dynamic Russian duo of sour cream and dill.

Russian bath

Building this Russian beauty is a laborious and complex process. Tradition dictates that the outer walls should be made of round pines or firs, preferably from the northern regions. There, the wood grows slowly and has a greater density, so it does not release as much resin when heated. The next important element is the red-hot stove or so-called "kamenka", which creates the special cozy, invigorating heat of the Russian bath. An authentic Russian bath does not need additional ventilation - a small hole in the ceiling is enough, from where the moisture quickly evaporates, and the wooden walls allow it to "breathe" without straining the heart and lungs like a sauna. They say that inside you feel like a mother's womb, ready to sweat out all the bitterness and disappointments of existence.

At one time, all significant events in a person's life took place here - the birth, the "wedding" bath of the newlyweds (the Russian proverb says that if a couple sweats together, they will grow old together) and that last one... The birch and juniper panicles with which the bathers apply boldly on the shoulders, make a pleasant massage with essential oils in their pure form, which delicately adhere to the skin and saturate the air with their vapors. So the experience is both relaxing and energizing. Let's not forget the accompanying pleasures - as soon as you come out of the bath refreshed, a royal feast awaits you with vodka and herring, Kiev cutlets, sturgeon, borscht, solyanka, pelmeni and blinis, abundant flights with strong tea from the singing samovar... Which reminds us that the Russians drank tea long before Mr. Twining opened his famous London shop and introduced the tradition of 5 o'clock tea to the British!

IN THE FOOTSTEPS OF OTTOMAN CUISINE

"Don't dismiss the meal as just food. For in itself this blessed creation is a whole civilization."
- Abdulhak Sinasi

Who could resist culinary temptations with such poetic names as lady's navel, belle's thigh, imam fainted or vizier's finger? But these delicacies, along with our well-known shish kebabs, Turkish coffee, baklava and Turkish delight, pilafs, sarmi and pistachios, are only the top of the minaret... Ottoman cuisine is a kind of culmination of an era saturated with drama, mysticism, rise and fall . From a culinary point of view, it marks the beginning of a new era, combining dozens of regional dishes and flavors, technological innovations and exotic spices and cooking techniques. It is amazing that at that time the Sultan's cooks held a single exam, namely the preparation of the simplest rice dish - pilaf. But it's just not easy... An established policy in the Sultan's palace was the selection of chefs from all corners of the empire, who enriched the menu with exotic dishes, experimented and created new recipes, which first passed through the palate of chesnijibashi (tasters), who tried the food of taste and checked for poison before admitting it to the table of the sultan and his family. The cooks in the Sultan's kitchen experimented with incredible ingredients and combinations, combining the culinary traditions of the peoples of Anatolia, the Crimea, the Balkans and the Middle East.

The classic age of the Ottoman Empire came in the 15th century, when Suleiman the Magnificent ascended the throne. But in order to gain insight into the Ottoman culinary culture and the recipes that are part of the modern lexicon of Turkish cuisine, we must delve into the ancestors of the Ottoman Empire.

The thread of history takes us to the Turkic nomadic tribes of Central Asia, who in the 7th-8th century settled in Anatolia. Dried salted meat, goat cheese prepared in goat skins and fermented mare's milk (koumiss) are some of the foods of these ancient peoples that remain in Central Asian cuisine today. It is believed that a characteristic culinary feature of Anatolia is the preparation of stuffed vegetables and birds, which has become a basic cooking technique not only in Turkish cuisine, but also in Balkan and Middle Eastern traditions.

Islam, the Arabic and Persian thread

In the 9th century, the Arabs conquered the Persian Samanid Empire and extended their dominions to central Asia. The teachings of the Prophet Muhammad (570-632) became that unifying force that contributed to the birth of Muslim culture with its distinctive features: large cities, mosques, charitable institutions, hospitals, kitchens for the poor, madrasahs, and so on. Islam prioritizes a sense of religious community and tolerates ethnic and linguistic differences while encouraging sensual pleasures and the physical, sensual and poetic enjoyment of food.

By 1054, the Seljuk Turks had already conquered much of the Middle East and had taken over the Arab dominions in Anatolia. Along with Islam, the Turks adopted from the Arabs and Persians many elements of their sophisticated urban culture, form of government, standing army, and court manners.

The classical Ottoman era

In 1453, the "followers of Osman" conquered Constantinople and renamed it Istanbul. The flowering of Ottoman culture occurred in the era of Rum Seljuk (1446 – 1566), that is, the empire of Suleiman the Magnificent, which extended over the territory of the Byzantine Empire. There are guilds, specialized markets, caravanserais and inns, and citizens can count on a constant supply of goods, food products of guaranteed quality and affordable prices. The three key elements necessary for the emergence of a fine culinary tradition are present. First of all, a fertile environment. Thanks to its location, regional diversity and territory, the empire has an inexhaustible abundance of food and products. The legacy of the imperial Byzantine cuisine offers hundreds of well-trained chefs specializing in the preparation of various types of dishes worthy of the Sultan's discerning palate. The palace kitchen, subject to a complex social organization, rich urban life, specialization of labor, intensive trade and complete control over the ancient Spice Road, reflect the culmination of wealth and cultural flourishing in the capital of the mighty Ottoman Empire. But apart from all this, Turkish cuisine has the privilege of developing at the crossroads between the Far East and the Mediterranean, reflecting the long and complex history of the migration of Turkic tribes from the Asian steppes to Europe.

The Sultan's Kitchen

The palaces in Istanbul and Edirne each had two kitchens, the kitchen of the ruler and his family (matbah humayun) and a kitchen for everyone else who resided in the palace (matbah amir). The kitchens of Topkapı Palace are populated by a staff of several hundred to several thousand highly specialized cooks, assistants and apprentices who feed the ten thousand palace residents with two main meals and one afternoon snack. A separate branch of recipes, zeitinals, i.e. dishes with olive oil, is being developed. These are dishes with pulses, legumes or vegetables that are cooked with only olive oil and served at room temperature. Tatlja confectioners are a separate class among palace chefs. They are engaged in the preparation of halvis, majoons, sherbets and all kinds of syrupy sweets, even perfumed soaps, and are known as helvajian-hassa (the sultan's halwajis).

Like beads on the thread of life

All significant events in life, from births, circumcisions, marriages and funerals, are celebrated with strictly defined meals and foods. After giving birth, the mother was given apricot nectar or sherbet with pink-tinted cinnamon sugar to help her recover. The circumcision ceremony was accompanied by lavish celebrations marking the young man's entry into the Muslim community. Wedding Clear Lamb Soup and Bridal Red Lentil Soup are two dishes that are served to this day. One of the most ancient dishes, ashure, became a culinary masterpiece in the Ottoman era. It is prepared in the tenth lunar month and contains all kinds of cereals and pulses that Noah was able to save after the end of the Flood.

A Handful of authentic recipes

Pekmez is an aromatic, slightly caramelized grape syrup. According to the ancient method, which is still used today, white huma (pekmez toprağı) is added to the syrup before it is boiled, which acts as a clarifying agent. Philip Addison, one of the organizers of the Oxford Culinary Symposium, describes pekmez in his book Pages from the Turkish Notebook:

"The grape juice is boiled down to a thick sugar syrup. It ranges in color from amber brown to almost black, and is an excellent source of grape sugar. In winter it is sold in wooden ducks and eaten for breakfast. At first it has the consistency of thick honey, but at room temperature it softens to a thick, incredibly delicious liquid that is drunk in the winter as a tonic against colds.'

Another popular drink is shira. In 1525, the Holy Roman ambassador to the court of Suleiman the Magnificent, Ogier Ghislain de Busbecq, described the preparation of shira in his famous Turkish Letters:

"The grapes are crushed and ground, then poured into a wooden vessel. They pour water in a strict ratio and mix carefully, then cover the container and leave the mixture to ferment for two days. If you taste it at the beginning of fermentation, you will find it unpleasant and excessively sweet; but after a while it acquires a sour taste, and if mixed with something sweet, it is very pleasant to the palate. It is drunk cold with snow, which you can always get in Constantinople.'

A favorite treat served to the Sultan on the fifteenth day of the holy month of Ramadan to mark the halving of fasts was soanlu yumurta or eggs with onions. The recipe is quite simple and will probably please the followers of the slow food movement (Slow Food) to no end, but it has its subtleties. Finely chop half a dozen sweet onions, salt and caramelize with butter over low heat in a shallow pan. The mixture should be simmered for three hours until it becomes a thick paste. Then the cook added a few drops of vinegar, two spoons of sugar, a pinch of pepper and waited a little longer. Finally, with the handle of the wooden spoon, he opened several pockets and knocked half a dozen fresh eggs into them, covered the pot and left the dish to simmer for another ten minutes. Soganli yumurta is served generously sprinkled with black pepper and cinnamon. And don't worry, you don't have to cook the treat for three hours, you can do it the quick way, unless you're planning to take the palace chef exams... Another popular drink is shirat. In 1525, the Holy Roman ambassador to the court of Suleiman the Magnificent, Ogier Ghislain de Busbecq, described the preparation of shira in his famous Turkish Letters:

The grapes are crushed and ground, then poured into a wooden vessel. They pour water in a strict ratio and mix carefully, then cover the container and leave the mixture to ferment for two days. If you taste it at the beginning of fermentation, you will find it unpleasant and excessively sweet; but after a while it acquires a sour taste, and if mixed with something sweet, it is very pleasant to the palate. It is drunk cold with snow, which you can always get in Constantinople.

A favorite treat served to the Sultan on the fifteenth day of the holy month of Ramadan to mark the halving of fasts was soanlu yumurta or eggs with onions. The recipe is quite simple and will probably please the followers of the slow food movement (Slow Food) to no end, but it has its subtleties. Finely chop half a dozen sweet onions, salt and caramelize with butter over low heat in a shallow pan. The mixture should be simmered for three hours until it becomes a thick paste. Then the cook added a few drops of vinegar, two spoons of sugar, a pinch of pepper and waited a little longer. Finally, with the handle of the wooden spoon, he opened several pockets and knocked half a dozen fresh eggs into them, covered the pot and left the dish to simmer for another ten minutes. Soganli yumurta is served generously sprinkled with black pepper and cinnamon. And don't worry, you don't have to cook the treat for three hours, you can do it the quick way, unless you're planning to take the palace chef exams...

TWENTY FLAVORS FROM BULGARIA - WHAT, WHERE AND HOW

Rich, natural, fresh, rich and aromatic - this is the taste of Bulgaria. Thanks to the location and history of the country - the cradle of the Thracian wine culture in the center of the Balkans, on the threshold of the Orient and in the middle of the land kissed by all the goddesses of fertility, the Bulgarian culinary tradition combines the best of Slavic, Greek, Turkish cuisine and even the saddlebags of the ancient equestrian peoples of Central Asia. Many dishes, as their names suggest, are borrowed from Turkish Ottoman cuisine, which in turn draws inspiration from Greece, the Crimea and the Caucasus. The flattering rays of the sun, the crystal clear spring water, the proud power of the mountain and the mischievous sea winds give a special flavor that makes Bulgarian dishes unforgettable.

The twenty legendary flavors that we present here are conditionally divided into four categories - sea, mountain, merry table and sweet delights. Approach them with a healthy dose of imagination and experiment and combine with a brave heart - so far there is no known way to go wrong. It is even possible to create your own unique menu and bouquet of flavors to take with you and turn into an exotic addition to your usual table.

Cheers!

Black Sea delights

Tarator - Addictively delicious cold yogurt soup, finely chopped cucumber, dill, crushed walnuts, crushed garlic and delicate pearls of sunflower oil or olive oil floated to the surface. A few years ago, a celebrity chef (master chef) created a standing ovation at a global culinary competition by turning tarator into a frozen appetizing sorbet. There is no better way to lighten up and cool down in the summer heat and midday haze at the seaside. A strong friendship connects the tarator with the next finalist in our ranking, namely mastic.

Mastika - a high-alcohol aniseed drink from the family of ouzo, perno and pastisa, which is usually drunk very chilled ("in crystals") and with a few drops of water or ice, which turn it from clear to a milky white fragrant liquid. The legendary sea cocktail "cloud" is obtained by adding a few sips of mint liqueur to the mastic, forming a serene aromatic ambrosia that is capable of invigorating even the most sun- and seawater-sucked vacationer.

Tarama caviar – another faithful friend of the above combination. It is well beaten with oil, lemon juice, ethereal onion puree and fish roe in the middle of a slice of dry bread. An appetizing, unpretentious appetizer that can't match the aristocratic sophistication of caviar, but it deserves to be tried.

Black Sea fish - turbot, lefer, saffron, if possible caught before sunrise and prepared by the skilled hands of the local hostess. From Nessebar in the south, they serve the fish fried until golden or toasted on the grill with skordalia - a spicy garlic paste, or with a dressing of vinegar, garlic and devesil. The student version of these delicacies is the magical combination of "fried sprats and fries" - the tiniest, undersized Black Sea fish sold in the cheerful traps along the shore and accompanied by countless pints of draft beer.

Grapewine sarmi with yogurt - lean or with a little minced meat, the dish is found with certain variations in Greek, Turkish, Armenian, Jewish and Lebanese cuisines, but the key factor in the Bulgarian recipe is the size (as big as a child's thumb), the aromatic spices (fennel, parsley, chives and spring onions), the silky fine vine leaves from the asma in the hostess's yard and the dill and garlic yogurt sauce with which they are served.

Mountain flavors

With the full awareness that the culinary traditions of Pirin, the Rhodopes and Stara Planina (the Balkans) are quite different, we bet on the leading element and the desire for hearty, nutritious dishes that warm the bones of the frozen traveler and ignite his blood for new snowy adventures.

Bean salad - a typical winter, nutritious salad of ripe beans (preferably Smiljanski), chopped onions, roasted red peppers and homemade lutenica. Able to satiate starving vegetarians and whet the appetite of mountaineers.

Patatnik – a specific regional recipe from the Rhodopes, which is a patty with a local variety of potatoes, with a lot of butter, cheese and jodgen. Interestingly, the dish is not prepared in an oven, but on a sach – a round clay plate with a rim at the end, placed on the embers in the oven.

Lamb chomlek kebab - one of those tender and aromatic meat dishes that are prepared in a clay pot (pot, casserole or pitcher) and are a typical representative of the "slow food" movement, simmering for hours on low heat. Interchangeable with kaverma kebab or the famous Banska Kapama, which, in addition to three types of meat, also includes sausage or blood sausage, sauerkraut, red wine and aromatic herbs and spices.

Lamb cheverme - Bulgarians jokingly call the days around the feast of Saint George (May 6) "the silence of the lambs". And they honor the patron saint of fighters, shepherds and shepherds with a freshly slaughtered whole animal - a lamb, a goat or a kid, which is roasted on a grill, in an oven or stewed in a dug pit. The cooking lasts at least 5-6 hours, until the meat is evenly baked to a golden crust, constantly basting it with its own fat, and in some regions with honey. The experience and taste of the meat is unforgettable under the shade of ancient trees and in combination with the intoxicating red wine.

Red wine - a stay in the lands of the Thracians, the most sophisticated wine culture of antiquity, would not be complete if you did not try at least a few types of wine from the unique local grape varieties. Trust your own intuition or the sommelier's advice and enjoy the divine properties of Merlot, Cabernet Sauvignon, Ruby, Mavruda, Pamida and Gamzata.

Merry table

Shop salad - white and as if covered in snow on the outside, colorful and delicious on the inside, this salad has been around for decades as the culinary business card of Bulgaria. Its name suggests that it is typical of the region around Sofia, called shoplak. The authentic Shop salad includes roasted red peppers, finely chopped fresh onions, garden cucumbers and tomatoes, lots of parsley and a thick covering of grated white cheese as dense as the snow cover of Vitosha. Even if you fall in love with it, be sure to try its less famous, but equally delicious sisters - Dobrudzha, Ovarska, Kalugera and Snezhanka. Always an appetizer with the Bulgarian grape or plum brandy.

Wolf appetizer - behind this euphemism lies an unimaginable variety of cold meat appetizers - dried goat and beef pastrami, various sudzuks and sausages, banski starets, venison fillet, sheep sazderma... Some of them are produced according to a traditional, kept secret recipe, others are typical for a given region and even a city (Ban old man is made only in Bansko, and Veliko Tarnovo, Gorna Oryahovitsa and Karlovo compete for the championship in making the tastiest sudjuci and lukanki).

Pogacha - puffy, fragile and irresistibly delicious bread, on which the skillful hands of the hostess sculpt fabulous scenes with birds, flowers and braids. In some regions, you will be served tutmanik or milinki instead of the bread. With them, every dish becomes tastier, and separately, served with cheese, merudia (colored salt) or honey for breakfast, they are able to keep you full all day.

Banitsa - another trademark of Bulgarian cuisine. It is truly lucky to taste an authentic grandmother's pie with crusts specially rolled out by some stooped old woman in the village, with eggs just laid by the chickens in the yard and a filling of white cheese, spinach or pumpkin. But given the circumstances - authentic Bulgarian grandmothers are becoming less and less - you can trust the works of good pastry chefs and bakeries.

Rakia - although they do not call their national alcoholic drink by such poetic names as "water of life" or "water of fire", Bulgarians are ready to suffer and rise up in defense of this spiritualizing liquid. No amount of administrative regulations and regulations managed to eradicate the tradition of home brandy brewing, although the colorful copper cauldrons became invisible. Any self-respecting Bulgarian will pull out of the deep reserves a bottle of thick, amber hot brandy to stun a guest. Each region is proud of its unique drink - Trojan plum, Burgas grape, Silistren apricot and even Karlovo rose rakia...

Sweet Temptations

Most traditional sweet delights are borrowed directly from Turkish cuisine - syrupy delights such as baklava, revane and tolumbicki, others are simple but unfathomably delicious desserts, and there are also such masterpieces that have appeared in one place for unknown reasons, why and when in the country, becoming a legend for generations.

Sheep yogurt with a garnish of honey and walnuts, blueberry jam or green or ripe fig jam. Explanations are unnecessary here, the combination of the dense, perfectly balanced taste of the thick yogurt and the ethereal sweetness of the jam gives the perfect dessert after a hearty meal or as a light snack on hot summer days.

Katmi - thick, porous pancakes, which are prepared on a clay pot over an open fire and eaten abundantly garnished with blueberry jam, honey or liquid chocolate. A divine taste that is punished with thousands of calories.

Damgi - an apocryphal dessert that is made only in Sozopol, crispy lacy sweets in the shape of a wheel of cheruk according to a recipe secretly brought from the court of the Byzantine Vasilevs, as the legend goes.

White jam - another forgotten aromatic delight that is present in the childhood memories of most Bulgarians. There are at least three recipes for a thick sticky confection of this name, which is served scooped up with a spoon and dipped in a glass of water, a fixture at ladies' gatherings from the late 19th to mid-20th century. In the authentic version, the secret agent in the recipe is chuven root, but in its modern version, the white jam is made from glucose, sugar, egg whites, lemon juice and essence.

Baklava, tatlis and saralias – classic oriental pastries with walnut filling, richly soaked in sugar syrup. If you're watching your figure, it's best to replace them with fresh fruit from some grandfather's garden at the market - the sweet, cooling core of ripe watermelon, honeydew melon crescents, sticky-sweet figs, heady apricots and peaches will fill you up without guilt. And they will inspire you to enjoy life!

CULINARY CONQUEST: BARCELONA, VALENCIA AND MADRID

SPANISH CUISINE IS a remarkable transformation of simple products such as onions, garlic, peppers, green spices, sage and olive oil into incredibly tasty and varied dishes. In fact, one cannot speak of a Spanish national cuisine, because it synthesizes the culinary traditions of the numerous regions of the kingdom. Historically, it takes the best of the gastronomic habits of the Romans, the Moors and the South American Indians. But in defiance or in honor of culinary stereotypes, in Spain one must try the famous Valencian paella, the cooling gazpacho, the filling tortilla, the blue cheese Cabrales, the national delicacy jamón and the cult liquid chocolate churros. Let's not forget the wine - Spain produces over a hundred brands of wine, not counting sherry and Madeira...

Tapas and cañas in Barcelona

When you enjoy the beauties of the Catalan capital and walk around the remarkable creations of Antonio Gaudí and Luis Domenech y Montaner, who marked architectural modernism with masterpieces such as the magnificent Sagrada Familia cathedral, the residential building La Pedrera that comes to life in the wind, the incomparably beautiful concert hall (Palau de la Musica Catalana) and the cheerful porcelain mosaics in Park Güell, you can ride the waves of the afternoon siesta with a glass of vermouth or beer and some tapas.

Tapas and Cañas is a great way to get up close and personal with the Spanish culinary tradition without overeating. The "tapas" are small bites that are served in most Spanish bars with the ordered drink, a kind of compliment from the establishment. The classic formula is tapas y cañas, that is, snacks and beer in small water glasses. There are different legends about the origin of tapas. In Seville, it is said that the morning breakfast of the bullfighters consisted of a glass of sherry topped with a piece of jamon. According to another version, in bars, they protected the drink from the crawling insects by covering it with a small saucer, in which they put something small to eat, necessarily spicy and salty, to ignite the thirst for a second drink. The size and type of tapas varies by region and restaurant, but throughout Spain you can safely skip dinner if you plan to go out for drinks. Just ask for the best tapas bars in town. In the northern regions (Asturias, Cantabria and Navarre) they serve pinchos (pinchos or pintxos in the Basque Basque language), that is "spikes" because they are usually served "pierced" with a toothpick. In Ávila, Segovia and Cáceres they serve warm tapas - croquettes, baguettes, squid and tortilla. The tapas plates are usually shared between friends and fellow diners so that everyone can try everything. Just ask for algo para picar (literally "something to poke/bite") or una ración if you want a larger portion.

The choice most often includes jamón, a raw cured ham, with the two deli options jamón serrano ("mountain ham") and the more expensive jamón ibérico de bellota (from an Iberian breed of pig fed only acorns), often called pata negra, meaning black thigh; externally, the thighs differ in the color of the hoof (white in Jamon Serrano and black in Iberico); followed by the famous Catalan sausages llangonisseta and fuet; aceitunas or olivas – olives; patatas bravas: literally bold potatoes, that is, fries with hot sauce; queso manchego: hard sheep's milk cheese; chorizo a la sidra: chorizo made with apple wine; pulpo a la gallega: boiled octopus seasoned with olive oil and hot red pepper; pimientos de Padrón: small green peppers fried in olive oil; calamares a la romana: breaded squid rings; boquerones: fresh anchovies marinated in vinegar and served with garlic and parsley;

gambas al ajillo: fried shrimp with garlic; salpicón de marisco /pulpo en vinagre: marinated octopus with chili peppers, tomatoes and onions.

A great place to try tapas and immerse yourself in Barcelona's vibrant energy is Bar Pinotxo in the famous indoor market Mercat de la Boqueria (Rambla no. 91, Mercat de la Boqueria) or Cuines Santa Caterina in the Halles Santa Caterina, a building in itself is an icon of Catalan architecture (#cuinessantacaterina, Av. de Francesc Cambó no. 16).

If you prefer a real Catalan dinner in the heart of the old town, choose Los Caracoles, which, despite its misleading name ('snails'), offers great seafood paella and typical lamb and pork dishes, all at very reasonable prices. The setting is rustic and the restaurant is very popular with Barça residents, so it's a good idea to make a reservation.

Paella in Valencia

THE THIRD LARGEST CITY in Spain and the capital of the autonomous region of Valencia beckons the traveler with enchanting charm, beautiful beaches, fire-breathing celebrations, beautiful architecture and delicious specialties. The Old Town owes its magical atmosphere to the exquisite tangle of historical and architectural influences imprinted on the winding maze of narrow streets. In the two proud squares, Plaza de la Reina and Plaza del Ayuntamiento, you will find welcoming restaurants and bars where you can try the famous Valencian paella (the correct pronunciation is paeya), which is undoubtedly at its best in its hometown during the explosive March festivities of Las Fayas (Les Falles or Las Fallas), when Valencians drive away winter and evil forces with lavish fireworks and faya sculptures, reflecting or rather mocking the iconic figures and events of the past year.

The classic Valencian paella is prepared in a special pan (paellera) and, in addition to rice, olive oil and saffron, includes chicken, green beans, tomatoes, peas, and often seafood and other types of meat. Tradition dictates eating with a wooden spoon straight from the pan, but modern restaurants do not insist on this typical feature. La Riuá Restaurants (La Riuá, Calle del Mar No. 27) has a central location, a traditional setting and a rich menu at affordable prices. The School of Rice and Paellas (Escuela de arroces y paellas, Calle Juristas No. 12) is close to Valencia Cathedral and offers typical dishes. You can't go wrong if you visit the central malls (Mercat Central de València) and support yourself with tapas at the Central Bar or at one of the small bistros nearby, offering fresh fried sardines and other delicious traditional "fast" or "slow" delicacies.

In Valencia, be sure to try the divine pastries with a palpable oriental flavor, heritage from the Moors. Although the trademark of Valencia is the Turrón nougat, prepared from honey, sugar and egg whites, with roasted almonds and other nuts, the similarities with the white halva that spins on a thread and breaks seals according to Zagovezni are too distinct... Therefore, more have a good bite of Suspiro de Monja - ethereal lemon-scented donuts that are still made in convent bakeries to this day, the richly honey-soaked Torrijas or the irresistible churros with liquid chocolate (chocolate con churros).

Enrich your taste experience with a glass of horchata, a white, almond-milk-like drink made from the chufa (Cyperus esculentis), also known as ground almond. The plant was brought to Spain by the Moors and, according to Spanish scientists, is the food of the future. If you prefer a stronger aperitif, go to one of the bars in the Plaza de la Virgen and order the "Agua de Valencia" - a cocktail of sparkling cava wine, gin, vodka and freshly squeezed juice from Valencian oranges, which, like sangria, served in a large glass pitcher.

Evening in Madrid

And when you tire of wandering among the splendor of the imperial capital, starting from the "zero kilometer" of the Puerta del Sol and heading to the districts of old Madrid, the Palacio Real Palace and the Plaza de Cibeles, the bars, museums, trendy shops and clubs of the revived Malasaña districts and Chueca, Rastro's treasure trove of kitsch and charming trinkets, try some of the city's signature dishes. Along the way, you can eat a breaded calamari sandwich (Bocadillo de Calamares) in the themed bars of the Plaza Mayor, with a glass of beer and a garnish of shiny, delicious olives. Or support yourself with traditional Galician and Extremadura empanadas – delicious patties filled with vegetables, cheese, meat or fish. Another traditional dish hidden under the name "broken eggs" (Huevos Rotos) is a mountain of fried potatoes topped with an almost soft egg, sometimes with a side of toast, a few rings of chorizo or another spicy sausage for color and flavor. Cocido Madrileño is a thick stew of pork, vegetables, chickpeas and chorizo that simmers on low heat for a minimum of four hours and warms the traveler on windy winter evenings. Grilled pig's ears (Oreja a la Plancha) is a favorite appetizer, served on a large communal platter, liberally sprinkled with salt, hot paprika and sometimes freshly squeezed lemon juice (Casa Camacho, San Andrés #4, Malasaña). In Madrid it is worth trying the smoked tuna (Mojama). The word "mohamma" comes from the Arabic "musama", that is dry, but the specialty probably has a Phoenician origin, from the ancient Kadir (today's Cadiz), the first settlement of the Western Mediterranean. The Phoenicians salted the fish (most often the fillet) in sea salt for two days, then washed it and left it to dry in the open air for 15-20 days. Iconic Madrid bars, always packed with hearty, loud Spaniards, are El Tigre.

Tips for culinary adventurers

Portions in Spanish restaurants and cafes are huge, which explains the existence of the concept of "half portion" (media ración). It's a good idea to split the portion so that you have the opportunity to try more delicacies.

In Barcelona, not far from the Plaza de España, there is a tapas bar Tickets - La Vida Tapa, where you can taste the classic at first glance and profoundly avant-garde creations of Ferran Adrià, the maestro of molecular cuisine and the virtuoso of flavors who brought the culinary art of a whole new level. Here, the round shiny 'olives' are made from olive mousse, olive oil, lemon zest, cumin, black pepper, cinnamon and anise. The pistachios are fried in tempura; the crispy grisinis around which the jamon is wrapped is hollow and filled with lard... The atmosphere is light, soulful, sensual and exciting, predisposing to breaking boundaries and conventions.

GERMAN CUISINE

What is the secret ingredient of prosaic German cuisine that inspired geniuses such as Roentgen, Born, Herz, Hegel, Kant, Nietzsche, Schopenhauer, Goethe, Heine, Schiller, Hesse, Brecht, Beethoven, Mozart, Schubert and Wagner? Isn't it some trick of the culinary muse? Hardly... A logical explanation for the correlation between the constellation of distinguished scientists, philosophers, poets, writers and musicians and the nourishing delicacies of German gastronomy is found in the five basic values in the German psyche: the love of order (die Ordnungsliebe), the observance of laws (Befehl ist Befehl , literally an order is an order), meticulous diligence, precision (Pünktlichkeit) and frugality (Sparsamkeit).

In fact, the most characteristic feature of German cuisine is its diversity, the abundance of regional specialties and customs rooted in Germany's imperial history. But wherever you end up, be sure to try the weisswurst, the pork knuckle Eisbane, the Berlin roll (toasted bacon stuffed with pork tenderloin and prunes, served with a side of green peas, potatoes and fritters), Hamburg steak, Sauerbraten (beef marinated in wine and vinegar, which is served fried in butter with vegetables, ginger, apples, raisins and beetroot syrup). Each region has its own culinary trademark. In Bavaria, it's white sausages with sweet mustard, roast pork, dumplings, salty pretzels and sauerkraut. In Franconia – Nuremberg sausages, gingerbread and pasta (spatzle, schulfnüdeln and maulhachen). In the Black Forest, try chives (Zwiebelkuchen) and smoked ham, in Cologne – fragrant almond cakes, in Hamburg – fried sole, smoked fish, eel and shrimp soup. The famous specialties of Saxony are dishes with shrimp and vegetables and the Dresden Christmas cake, in Thuringia - the roast goose with dumplings. Breakfast (Fruehstuck) consists of cheese, sausages, eggs, muesli, bread, butter and jam. At midday (Mittagessen) a hot meal is served. Dinner (Abendbrot) is at 7pm and as the name suggests ("evening bread") usually consists of salad, bread, cheese and cold cuts.

And yet, who is the protagonist? The sausages? Sauerkraut? The beer? According to the English, this is the cabbage, so they sometimes call the Germans krauts. Yes, cabbage is an important actor, but not only. In Berlin's pubs and cafes, not far from Arkonaplatz, be sure to try the traditional Berlin cutlet (Kotelett) or meatballs (Klops) with potato salad, currywurst and a pint of beer. Ladies can try the combination of apple-almond strudel or apricot streusel and a pint of white beer (Berliner Weisse) with raspberry syrup.

The magic word is wurst

Today, over 1,500 types of sausages and sausages are sold in Germany: boiled, smoked, blood sausage, liver sausage, ham, sausages and sausages... no family celebration, picnic, bazaar or exhibition is complete without grilled sausages, unique to each region of the country, with a strictly prescribed recipe and regulated sizes. To this day, the recipes of many sausages are kept secret, as the popular saying dictates, "If you're going to die, you won't know what's in the sausage." For example, cumin is added to Thuringian sausages in addition to oregano, salt and pepper, white Bavarian (or Munich) sausages are eaten with a bun and sweet mustard, Coburg wursts can reach a length of 32 cm, while Nuremberg ones should not exceed 8-9 cm. The most popular is the cult Berlin Currywurst - sliced pork sausage, generously garnished with ketchup and curry sauce, served with potato salad or bread. The "mother" of the currywurst is believed to be Herta Hoever, owner of a street diner in the Charlottenburg district of West Berlin. She began preparing the delicacy in 1949 to feed the influx of construction workers rebuilding destroyed Berlin, and in 1959 patented the spicy sauce under the name Chilliup. Herta Hoever's diner operated until 1974, and the resourceful lady and her delicious specialty are immortalized with a memorial plaque and a museum (Deutsches Currywurst Museum). It is worth trying the smoked

Westphalian ham on the bone, with a slight scent of juniper berries, which the Romans still appreciated, the frankfurters from Neu-Isenburg, the Black Forest ham, the white Munich sausages, which are traditionally eaten before the clock strikes noon... Where? At one of the countless stalls on the streets, especially if you see around you customers of all types and caliber - elegant clerks, construction workers, even politicians... before a wurst, everyone is equal.

Bread

"THERE IS NO REAL BREAD in America, and I love bread so much," Bertolt Brecht, who emigrated to the USA, wrote in his diary. In Germany, more than 300 different types of bread and 1,200 types of buns and rolls are produced, most of them whole grain, from the "soul" of the grain, as the Germans poetically express it. Typical German bread is made from rye-wheat flour, often combined with oats, barley, spelled, seeds and spices, onions, walnuts, even peas and carrots. The further south-west you go, i.e. the closer you get to France, the whiter and puffier the sammunes become. On the other hand, in Westphalia you can try pumpernickel, the blackest black bread, made almost exclusively of coarse rye flour and bran, which is not baked, but steamed. Thus, the quarter mold remains compact, moist and durable, with a slightly sweet taste.

Be sure to try the authentic German pretzel with a brown, crispy salty crust and tender milky white flesh, fluffy in the middle and with thin but not dry "hands". Legend has it that the recipe for the original pretzel (Laugenbrezel) was the result of a mistake by a Bavarian master baker. On February 11, 1839, Anton Nepomuk Pfannenbrenner, the baker of the Royal Cafe in Munich, prepared sweet pretzels for the guests. Kanel tried to spread a sweet glaze on the ready-to-bake cows, but mistakenly picked up the bowl of weak sodium hydroxide solution that was used to clean the countertops. Although he realized the mistake, the master still decided to bake the pretzels, which came out of the oven with an unprecedented brown crust, soft interior and incredible taste. The guests were very satisfied, and the master gained unexpected fame. The shape of the pretzel is also shrouded in mystery. According to some sources, it derives from the shape of the Roman round loaves, others send us to the monasteries, where the shape of the pretzel was supposed to resemble a praying monk, with arms crossed on his shoulders. Famous are the large pretzels (Wiesnzeit), which are baked especially for Oktoberfest, with a light brown crust and a white interior that tastes like rustic white bread.

Beer

Although they did not invent beer, which was a favorite drink even in ancient Mesopotamia, entered the diet of the builders of the pyramids along the Nile, and in Greece was considered the drink of the common people, in Germany alone there are over 5,000 brands of beer and an official Day of German beer, which is celebrated on April 23 as a kind of reference to the Beer Purity Law of 1516, the world's oldest regulation in the field of the food industry and a source of pride for the German Brewers Guild. The law dictates that only four ingredients can be included in the composition of beer: water, hops, yeast and malt: "God save hops and malt!".

Listing all the styles of German beer is a daunting task, but the most basic categories are alt, bock (a strong beer that can be doppel bock, ice bock and heller bock), dunkel (try Münchener dunkel), export, adel (from special hop varieties), hel, kölsch, keller ("cellar beer"), lager, maltsbier, merzen ("March" beer), rauch (smoky beer), pils and the wheat weissbier. They differ in the ratio of ingredients, brewing temperature, alcohol content, degree of aging and taste.

The Riesling Renaissance

Did you know that in the 19th century, fine Rieslings from Rheinhau were among the most expensive wines in the world? Merchants in London sold a bottle of quality Riesling for more than

French Bordeaux. But after a dark period of decline, since the early 1990s Germany has seen a revival of the wine tradition. So if you like light white wines, be sure to try wine from the leading regions of Rheinhau (Weil, Kuenstler, Wgeuer), Mosel-Saar-Rover (Haag, Loosen, Pruem) or Palatinate (Doennhoff, Knipser, Mueller-Catoir).

What, where, when
Berlin

The annual Berlinale International Film Festival takes place during the second and third weeks of February. The Easter market around the Kaiser Wilhelm Memorial Church and on Alexanderplatz is usually in April. The theater festival, which flows into the youth theater festival, takes place from the middle to the end of May. The Traditional Music Festival and Bach Days are in early July every odd year (2015). The Mid-July Love Parade. October marks the holiday of German reunification. In November is the Jazzfest, which has been held since 1964. Four days of jazz concerts, performances by jazz groups and individual soloists.

To feel the atmosphere of Old Berlin, you can walk among the Hackesche Höfe (Hackesche Höfe) in the Mitte district, the largest complex of courtyards in Germany, which has been a national architectural monument since 1972. In Berlin, you can try fusion cuisine, tour great bars with live music and a bohemian atmosphere, see the work of avant-garde photographers and designers. It is useful to buy a Berlin WelcomeCard, which combines a ticket for all modes of transport for 48 or 72 hours and gives you a discount on entrances to all museums, city tours, some restaurants and bars.

Cologne

The Fastelovend carnival begins on November 11th at exactly 11.11am with a shrill cry of "Koele alaaf"! During this spectacular holiday, and especially in the days leading up to Pink Monday and Ash Wednesday, anything is permitted. The festivities begin with the "three crazy days" (which are actually five), the first of which is the women's carnival (viberfastnacht), the traditional parade of students and residents of the surrounding small towns on Sunday, and reaches its climax with Pink Monday.

Munich

The summer music festival. Nymphenberg Palace opens its doors for secular music festivals in the ceremonial Stone Hall.

And of course, Oktoberfest – the most popular 16-day beer festival, which takes place on the Theresienwiese square and gathers six million visitors each year (72% Bavarians and 15% tourists). The fest begins on the first Saturday after September 15 and ends on the first Sunday of October, or so as to include the day of German reunification. National celebrations, a sea of beer and abundant food, cheerful international companies, Bavarians in leather pants (Lederhosen) and blonde beauties in dresses with embroidered felt bibs (Dirndl) and countless toasts starting with ein Prosit! The most delicious beer from wooden barrels, of course, is offered by the Augustinian brewery. As is known, to this day a large part of the five thousand types of German beer is brewed by monks.

LONDON: TRADITIONS ARE IN FASHION

London Spring. That is, rain, fog and a biting wind. Gentlemen read The Times and eat a traditional breakfast: scrambled eggs, lightly browned bacon and a formidable nutritious side dish of roasted tomatoes, mushrooms, beans and bloodstains. More delicate natures have breakfast with oatmeal. Then the obligatory cup of English breakfast tea and a transparent slice of toast with orange jam. Welcome to good old England, the last bastion of etiquette, rules and traditions!

Dignity, composure, a pinch of snobbery and a generous dose of self-irony - these are the distinguishing features of a true Englishman. What is hell, asks a popular English anecdote? A place where the police are German, the comedians are Swedish, the cooks are Turkish, and the waiters are Irish... The monarchy is constantly criticized, but "God save the Queen"!

In my childhood, there were legends about the terrible English kitchen - heavy, sloppy and bland. The novels of Dickens and Sir Conan Doyle conjured up even darker images: outwardly indistinguishable sometimes meat, sometimes fruit puddings (we will dwell on these in detail later), shepherd's, country and fisherman's pies with startling flavors and ingredients, roast beef, fish and chips, on holidays some bloody steak with meat sauce gravy or mashed potatoes and bacon-wrapped sausages known as "Pigs in blankets", a typical delicacy at the Christmas table... In terms of drinking, things seemed somewhat more cheerful - the English understand from any beer, black ale is pure ambrosia, ladies support themselves with sherry and port, gentlemen drink whisky, brandy and rum. Gin is only for cockneys.

However, the reality is much tastier

As soon as you set foot in London, it becomes clear that whether thanks to the cultural richness of the colonial past, whether because of the liberal tolerance of the English, whether because of their traditional curiosity and the mixing of styles and gastronomic influences, English cuisine has experienced a culinary Reformation, and London has become in a world-class gourmet fusion capital. Modern restaurants offer a fantastic taste eclecticism, and the lively high streets are full of Moroccan, Sudanese, Thai and Indian restaurants beckoning with great temptations.

However, we go in search of tradition and come across the oldest restaurant in London, The Rules ("The Rules", 35 Maiden Lane, Covent Garden, WC2E 7LB, http://www.rules.co.uk/), opened in 1789 which offers aristocratic British cuisine and transports us to a setting worthy of Sir Arthur Conan Doyle. Moreover, Edward VII, King of Great Britain and Ireland, Emperor of India (1901 - 1910), first of the Saxe-Coburg-Gotha dynasty (later renamed Windsor), liked to have lunch here with his girlfriend, the actress Lily Langtree , at the neat "tables for two" in the belly of the hall, designed naturally for lovers and - oh wonder! – the most tightly engaged seats in the restaurant to this day! Charles Dickens, William Thackeray, Graham Greene, Clark Gable, Charlie Chaplin and other great personalities have dined here. The salon is spacious, the floor mosaic is colorful, the obligatory hunting trophies hang on the walls. The menu itself is an apotheosis of British culinary art: Windsor soup, partridge with walnut and apricot stuffing, smoked venison, smoked Scottish salmon, foie gras pate, special recipe roast beef and of course the full range of the timidly mentioned above pies and puddings.

This brings us to the original question: what is pudding?

At first glance, pudding is a dessert. From the shelves in the supermarket, we get the impression that the pudding is something like cream-malebi from the kindergarten, but with more shape and more taste. In good old England, however, pudding can be hot, meaty and hearty, such as Yorkshire beef and horseradish pudding. I will not dwell on the metaphorical use of the word (understand from a cheeky maiden to a pregnant maiden), as it deserves a separate story.

Back in the day, the housewives and cooks in the manors collected the remaining products, possibly after the preparation of the noble table or at all, and mixed them with whatever they could - hence such strange recipes as pudding with trifles, pigeons and prunes... but it's delicious, try it!

As for pies, London is the best place to try a banoffee pie

The creators of this famous pastry are Ian Dowding and Nigel McKenzie, respectively chef and owner of the cult restaurant "The Hungry Monk" (The Hungry Monk) in Jevington, East Sussex. They created the dessert in 1972, inspired by Blum's American coffee-caramel pie (Blum's Coffee Toffee Pie). Dowding adapted the recipe by replacing the caramel with reduced condensed milk, and McKenzie added the bananas. They call the creation "Banofi" and it instantly wins the hearts of customers. Annoyed by the banoffee-themed "free-forms" offered in hundreds of restaurants and supermarkets, in 1994 Mackenzie announced a £10,000 reward for anyone who could disprove his claim to authorship and discover a publication of the recipe before 1972. The original recipe was published in "The Deep Secrets of the Hungry Monk" in 1974 (the book is out of print) and in the following "On Seventh Heaven with the Hungry Monk" (1997). The Hungry Monk closed its doors in January 2012 due to "increased overhead costs" after running continuously for 44 years.

And we continue with the historical tour of the restaurants. And we arrive at the Gordon Ramsay - an emanation of style and snobbery, a celebrity frequented and noteworthy establishment, hailed as one of the best restaurants in the world and awarded three Michelin stars. Regarding the menu, it is a flight of fancy, from milk lamb in cream to duck breast with mushrooms and honey or venison in chocolate sauce...

Advice for adventurers

If you're not afraid of horrors like pickled eggs (a sinister-looking English specialty) and bad cholesterol, be sure to try:

Fish'n'Chips: the most popular dish in English cuisine. It is fried and breaded cod fish, which must be served with fried potatoes cut into slices. It is eaten liberally sprinkled with malt vinegar. Pea puree is also served with the dish. "Fish and chips" appeared in the mid-19th century as a workers' meal. The first fish and chip shop has opened in London. Today, in modern slang, these shops are known as 'chippies'.

If you visit London in winter, be sure to try the quintessential British Christmas specialty mince pie, literally mince pie. A filling of "mince" is poured onto a base of butter dough - a thick mixture of dried and candied fruits, grated apple, butter or sheep tallow and aromatic spices soaked in rum or cognac. The recipe has been part of British culinary tradition for centuries and originally did include meat, although today the only animal product in it is lard, often replaced by butter or vegetable fat. Another divine creation is the Caribbean or Creole Christmas cake - a chocolate cake with aromatic spices (nutmeg, cinnamon, cloves and vanilla), molasses, hazelnuts and dried fruits, which is soaked in a mixture of rum, brandy, cherry, port and Angostura bitters. It is prepared at least a week before the second day of Christmas ("the day of the boxes", when masters presented boxes full of treats and gifts to their servants) so that the spices develop and combine their flavors and aromas.

Hop over to Notting Hill if you want to immerse yourself in a real-time milieu of postmodern yogis, highlife loafers, Rastafarians and bohemians who swagger, take over, pose, spend and effervescence. You can also pop over to Portobello Road Market (the UK's largest antiques market, which also offers all sorts of other goods). The main market day is Saturday, and there are hundreds of vendors, located on stalls, in shops and bezis. The market is almost a kilometer long.

If you are lucky enough to stay in London for the weekend, take a walk to Camden Town, London's most youthful and colorful district, known as the mecca of eccentrics. Authors such as Charles Dickens,

George Orwell and Mary Shelley lived and worked here. There are several markets in the area, the most famous of which is Camden Lock.

Be sure to enjoy an authentic London pub with a twisted name, such as Percy's Earl or The Unicorn and the Hound, with the obligatory polished floorboards or shabby carpet, pool table and cardboard pork chop stand by the bar.

The Tabernacle pub is a living legend. A five-minute walk from Earl's Court tube station, the venue has been popular since the sixties and in its golden age has been adorned with countless record covers, becoming an arena for fashion photo shoots. But like an aging movie star that has lost its luster, today the bar has been forgotten by cutting-edge types and has become a favorite hangout for students and schoolchildren. Entering Tabernacle is like a trip to the Tyrolean Alps – plenty of apple strudel, pints of beer and merry laughter.

See the Shard Tower, a creation of Italian architect Renzo Piano. Western Europe's tallest building opened with a glittering ceremony on 5 July 2012, and its 87 floors house offices, apartments, expensive restaurants, galleries and an ultra-luxury hotel, towering over the nearby monumental St Paul's Cathedral in an insignificant church.

If you plan to spend more than two or three days in London, get yourself an Oyster card upon arrival - a plastic smart card that can be used instead of tickets on all types of public transport in London.

GEORGIAN WINES

The Georgian Caucasian wine-making tradition is a centuries-old practice that has deep cultural and historical significance. Situated at the crossroads of Europe and Asia, Georgia, located in the Caucasus region, is often regarded as the cradle of wine production. This ancient winemaking tradition has been recognized by UNESCO as an Intangible Cultural Heritage of Humanity.

European technology

Many saw how wine is made in Europe, some even participated. Entire festivals are held on this theme. The grapes are put in wooden tubs, crushed with bare feet, the juice is collected in containers and sent to ferment. That is, as a rule, only juice ferments. If the wine is red, then the skins are left, but the seeds and twigs are always removed - it is believed that they spoil the taste.

This is how it was done in ancient Greece, Rome, this is how wine is made in France now, and all other countries are guided by France. The consequence of this technology is a small extractiveness of the wine. Reduced astringency, more even flavor, without extremes. There are deviations, but mainstream wine is just that. In Georgia, Alexander Chavchavadze was the first to introduce this technology at his winery on the estate in Tsinandali.

According to this technology, Gurjaani, Napareuli, Manavi and Tsinandali wines are made in Georgia. These wines will be understandable and close to Europeans. However, this is a late development. Not as late as Coca-Cola, but still not ancient local.

Qvevri Winemaking

The traditional Georgian winemaking method revolves around the use of qvevri, large clay vessels buried underground. Grapes, including their skins, seeds, and stems, are placed inside the qvevri and fermented for an extended period, resulting in unique flavors and amber-colored wines. This method of winemaking has been practiced for over 8,000 years.

Kakhetian technology

We take grapes and crush it, turning it into porridge along with seeds and twigs. The resulting mass is poured into a large ceramic jug - qvevri. (Although it is not strictly required for this technology). Qvevri is dug into the ground, so it has a stable temperature - about 14 - 15 degrees. The wine material roams there for 3 or 4 months. That is, right with the skins, bones and twigs. For comparison, if the French insist on the skins of their Chardonnay, then no more than a week.

Then the liquid is drained and sent for storage. The chemical consequence of this technology is that a lot of extractive substances pass into wine from skins, seeds and twigs. The process is more complicated and mysterious than it seems. Coloring substances come from the skins into the juice, but under certain circumstances they can begin to be absorbed back into the skins.

The result - the taste is stronger, tart, rich. From a European point of view, this is a marginal, crude and wrong technology. If we take Burgundy wines as a sample, then Kakhetian wines are far from ideal. But in fact, they are just different samples. For Kakheti, an example of the right wine is Mukuzani.

But if you are familiar with winemaking, then it will be clear to you that the percentage of polyphenols in Kakhetian wines is much higher, and they are somewhat healthier. And the rougher, the better.

According to the Kakhetian technology, Saperavi, Mukuzani, Rkatsiteli, Tibaani, Kakheti, Sameba, Shuamta and some more are produced. I advise you to compare Mukuzani with Napareuli. The grapes are the same, the geography is approximately the same, but the technology is different. There are even wines made from Rkatsiteli grapes, made using two different technologies. In the first photo, a comparison of two technologies to visualize the difference. European technology on the left, where it is lighter, on the right - Kakheti. And wine - Rkatsiteli!

Imeretian technology

It is a cross between the first and second technologies. The wine material is infused a little less than Kakhetian - one and a half to two months. It is also infused with seeds and skins, but without twigs.

Result: about the same amount of alcohol, but higher acidity. Imereti wines are less tart, the taste is more even.

Wines made using this technology: Tbilisuri, Tsitska, Sviri, Dimi

Naturally semi-sweet wines should also be attributed to the same technology, but I'd rather put them separately.

Naturally semi-sweet wines

This method is originally Racha-Lechkhum. The essence of the method is that the grapes are harvested during a period of high sugar content, and then the wine ferments at a low temperature, about 4-5 degrees. It is cooler in Racha-Lechkhumi than in Kakheti, hence the special temperature regime. The wine ferments slowly, not all of the sugar is eaten by the yeast, and the wine is semi-sweet. In addition, slow fermentation contributes to the saturation of wine with carbon dioxide. These wines should be kept refrigerated and should also be drunk chilled. It's not champagne or sparkling wine, but there are bubbles.

There is a myth that semi-sweet wine is obtained by adding sugar to wine. It is not right. Such technology exists, and at one time it even flourished, but now only clandestine cattle factories or rural cattle farms do this. No one will allow wineries to mock wine materials like that.

If you have to drink semi-sweet wines, then you should keep in mind the fact that there are simpler technologies for its production, which, however, give worse quality. And we must also remember that naturally semi-sweet wines are not aged for long. If dry wines only improve from storage, then semi-sweet ones - on the contrary.

Historically, semi-sweet wines were made in the mountainous Racha, where the fermentation process was slowed down by natural cooling. Now the process is hampered by artificial refrigeration units. This is a very expensive pleasure, so at home it is irreproducible. If you are offered homemade semi-sweet - this is a reason to think.

The ideal of such a wine is Khvanchkara. Wines of the same type - Ojaleshi, Pirosmani, Tvishi, Alazani Valley, Akhasheni, Kindzmarauli, well, or the great Usakhelouri.

Storage

THIS IS NO LONGER A technology, but it is also very important. All major wine defects come from improper storage. There are several storage options. First. Draft wine is often stored in plastic bottles. This is acceptable if you intend to drink it today or tomorrow. But in 4-5 days, and in warm weather, any plastic wine will deteriorate.

The second way: glass bottles. The most classic and well-known

Third: ceramic bottles. Three years ago they were not, but now they are becoming more and more. There is no sense in such bottles, except for commercial ones. Marketers have written a lot of nonsense about these bottles, but the truth is that they are slightly better than plastic, but much worse than glass. Ceramics, alas, passes air, albeit very weakly. If such a bottle was taken to Russia for a long time, then stored somewhere for a long time, then you can be sure that the wine has already deteriorated. In theory, you can buy such a bottle (preferably immediately at the winery) and bury it in your dacha (provided that there are positive ground temperatures there in winter), and then it can be stored for a long time, but the question is - why?

There is another technological moment. In Europe, it is considered good form to make a specific wine from a specific grape. Saperavi from Saperavi. This method is partly rooted in Kakheti. But in the West of Georgia, mixing grape varieties is considered the norm.

Mystery

First. So, the right wine is the wine from the right grapes using the right technology. Such wine can be found in specialty stores or local wineries. It's expensive. But what do the peasants drink at home? It can be assumed that the correct Saperavi is grown in the village of Mukuzani, but who can guarantee the correctness of the technology? So, when you visit the residents of the village of Mukuzani, you will drink in general Mukuzani, but ... But still with some shades. This in itself is very interesting, but requires an understanding of the process.

Second. Traditionally, the wine is fermented and stored in a ceramic qvevri. Now more often use metal containers. On the one hand, the metal is easier to clean, it has less of any extraneous bacteria or mold. It is more modern and efficient. On the other hand, Qvevri is somehow more pleasant for the soul. Try some wines from different containers, try to feel the difference.

LISBON - THE CORNUCOPIA OF CULINARY ABUNDANCE

WELCOME TO LISBON, the westernmost capital of Europe. The old continent ends at Cape Cabo da Roca, less than 40 km from the Portuguese capital, plunging into the boundless waters of the Atlantic Ocean. The earthquake of 1755, followed by a fire and tsunami, deprived Lisbon of many historical landmarks, although thanks to the Marquis de Pombal, the city quickly rose from the ashes and ruins to captivate the imagination and senses of aesthetes and travelers. Magnificent churches, magnificent palaces and innumerable monuments to kings and marquises are constant reminders of Lisbon's imperial past and untold riches from the Age of Discovery.

The most important attributes of your adventure are comfortable shoes, a desire to saturate your senses with beauty, sounds, tastes and unfamiliar sensations, and also an insatiable appetite. Be prepared all day to wander the steep streets of the city, which often turn into stairs, to marvel at the divine blue azulejo tiles on the walls of buildings, to contemplate windows with patterned wooden shutters and laden with luxuriant begonias, miniature balconies decorated with proudly waving underwear, listening to fado and crying soul-cleansing tears, regardless of whether you understand Portuguese. Like many other magical cities, Lisbon is nestled in the gentle embrace of seven steep hills. Authentic and cozy, Lisbon amazes and fascinates at every turn. The neo-Gothic wrought iron lace of the 45-meter Santa Giusta elevator, which connects the shopping street to Piazza Carmo, from where you can admire the city from a bird's eye view and mark where to take, leaves the unforgettable feeling that you are traveling not only in the vertical of the city , but also back in time. The picturesque old quarter of Alfama seems to spill over the slopes below the castle of São Jorge with its cobbled streets, colorful facades, restaurants and markets. The smell of fried fish, the view of the enticing expanse of the ocean, the bars where port and fado are poured in the evening, are capable of stealing the heart of even the most hardened traveler. It is also worth seeing the "business card" of Lisbon - the Aguas Libres aqueduct, the wonderful Monument to the Discoverers - a stone ship that carried on board the great Portuguese navigators on a voyage through time and space, and the Belem Tower.

But wherever you go, the delicious aromas wafting in from all over, combined with the completely reasonable and affordable prices of the dishes, are able to turn a stay in Lisbon into a kind of culinary retreat that will revive your senses, emotions and soul. Because...

Because although it bears a certain resemblance to Mediterranean cuisine, traditional Portuguese cuisine is incomparably more attractive thanks to the abundance of exotic spices, a memory of the colonial era, when Prince Henri the Navigator ordered the captains of his flotilla to load the ships with all kinds of unknown fruits and spices from

The New World, thanks to which Europeans for the first time tasted tomatoes, potatoes and even tea, and knew the charm of piri-piri (horribly hot red peppers), black pepper, cinnamon and saffron.

For breakfast...Romeo and Juliet!

The gradation in the duration and abundance of the main dishes is interesting. Here, breakfast is light, but not simple - coffee, a roll or a slice of bread with... Romeo and Juliet! In Lisbon, the love story of the two lovers does not end tragically because here these words mean quince marmalade with a slice of mature cheese! The combination of the sweet and sour taste of the sun-baked marmalade and the slightly salty sheep's cheese is so beloved by the Portuguese that they often serve this literary snack as an appetizer or dessert.

For lunch ... "we have snails and other seafood"!

Dozens of cozy taverns (tascas) along the streets of Lisbon offer this delicacy (caracóis), especially in summer, when they wash it down liberally with ice-cold draft beer (imperiais). You must try bacalhau, that is, salt cod, which is celebrated as the backbone of the economy and the product that can be cooked in 365 different ways. Each region of Portugal has its own unique salt cod specialty. Prepared according to a 500-year-old recipe, bacalao is the most popular Portuguese appetizer. Small restaurants tempt the hungry traveler with an abundance of seafood delicacies delivered every morning from the Mercado di Ribeira – grilled sardines (sardinhas assadas), sea bass, stuffed squid, anchovies and swordfish, clams, prawns, oysters, lobsters and crabs... Another traditional dish is the fish stew Caldeirada, which is prepared from freshwater fish, sea fish and vegetables. The secret ingredient for the unique taste of caldeirada is the combination of white wine, olive oil and spices (piri-piri, black pepper, ginger and garlic), which are pre-mixed in a homogeneous ambrosia that gives the incredible taste. Served with lightly toasted bread.

If you prefer to support yourself quickly, stop at a kiosk (quiosque). These are charming little benches in the middle of the parks and around the main sights of Lisbon, which offer an idyllic setting for a light bite, coffee or cocktail. Here you can try fish soup (sopa de peixe) for less than 3 euros, a salt cod sandwich and a glass of young or as they say "green" wine (vinho verde) to be enjoyed while staring into the bustling life of the city.

If instead of having lunch you prefer to treat yourself to a Brazilian coffee and a pastry, enter a patisserie and taste ethereal delights that combine the best of the world. Prepared at the time in the monasteries by the tender fingers of nuns, the sweets were a means of providing additional income for the abode of God. The creations have exciting names such as the nun's navel (barriga de freira), angel breast (papos de anjo) and heavenly bacon (toucinho do céu). Try the divine lemon and cinnamon rice pudding (arroz doce) or sponge cake (pão de Ló) soaked in lemon and orange juice, Madeira, port and cinnamon. Or the legendary pastel de nata, which is served with a scoop of cinnamon ice cream. Lisbonians swear that this pastry must be tried nowhere else but at the famous pastry shop Pastéis de Belém (Rua Belém 84-92), built on the site of an early 19th-century sugar refinery. It is also worth taking a look at the oldest café in Lisbon, Café Martinho da Arcada (Praça do Comércio No. 3), which opened its doors in 1782. The famous poet Fernando Pessoa used to come here, so his favorite table awaits him to this day.

Dinner or repast

A typical Southern dinner starts late and lasts until midnight. After a tiring, action-packed day, you can support yourself with a traditional meal, abundant with different types of meat, beans, potatoes and spices (for example, cozido à Portuguesa or Feijoada, a slave stew of beans and trimmings brought from Brazil, a culinary spell for happiness and well-being), or pass by a tapas bar like the iconic Tágide (Largo da Academia Nacional de Belas Artes no. 18-20), housed in a lovely 18th-century building with dark wooden floors, walls of wine bottles and a view which takes your breath away, where you can eat green cream soup (caldo verde) or mussels in white wine and garlic (amêijoas à Bulhão Pato).

Cheese connoisseurs (queijo) can try the local goat and sheep milk specialties as an appetizer or instead of dessert. The most famous Portuguese sheep's cheese is Queijo da Serra, which is made in the Serra da Estrella region. It is prepared only in winter, and the milk is curdled with flor do cardo.

The best comes at the end: fado, porto, tears and soul catharsis
THE BEST PLACE TO DIVE into the deep waters of fate, love anguish and the nostalgic Portuguese soul is a small casa do fado in the narrow streets of the Muraria neighborhood, the birthplace of fado. Here the music flows spontaneously from the bars and improvised podiums in the middle of the street, here is also the oldest fado school for those who want to learn more about this magical art. Order your wine – whatever you choose, you won't go wrong – and get ready to cry your heart out with pure, soul-reviving tears, because whether you understand the lyrics or intuitively guess the plot of the song, the strings of the Portuguese guitar will touch your soul.

Wine has been made in these lands since time immemorial, more precisely since the golden ages of Hellas, Carthage and the Roman Empire. Northern Portugal is famous for its Douro vineyards and full-bodied, aromatic red wines. The most famous drink is probably port, which is usually served with dessert and has a rich, strong aroma. The subtlety in port production is the addition of brandy shortly before the fermentation process is complete. Madeira is another famous delicacy, which is practically port, which is heated to a temperature of 50 degrees Celsius for half a year.

Some of the best places for fado and wine are Café Luso (Travessa da Queimada #10), Clube de Fado (Rua de São João da Praça #92-94), O Faia (Rua da Barroca #54-56) and Sr . Vinho (Rua do Meio à Lapa

No. 18), where in an unpretentious (the first two) or an elegant traditional setting (the last two establishments) you will indulge in an incomparable and unforgettable experience.

For adventurers

A great idea is to take the "excursion" wooden tram 28, which goes around the most picturesque districts of Lisbon, or take a ride on the Bica iron funicular, a special type of cable tram that has become a kind of symbol of the city. Just by tram 28 you can reach the famous "thieves' market" Feira da Ladra in the Alfama neighborhood (open on Tuesdays and Saturdays), where historical souvenirs, exotic spices, jewelry and unpretentious antiques are sold.

Follow in the footsteps of the unique Manuelinho architectural style, which dates back to the mid-15th century and is named after King Manuel. The style is a magical mixture of Gothic, Moorish and exotic elements, and connoisseurs define it as the Portuguese Revival, as its heyday coincided with the supreme power of the kingdom. The most famous buildings in this style are the tower of Saint Vincent in Belen, the monastery in Batal, the royal residence in Sintra and the Lisbon Cathedral.

The name of the shopping mall is... Freeport and Campera! Freeport is located in the picturesque town of Alcochete, twenty minutes from the center of Lisbon, offering a combination of beautiful nature, authentic architecture and a paradise of designer shops. A shuttle bus runs twice a day in both directions. Campera Outlet Shopping is the first factory outlet center in Portugal, one of the largest in Europe. The concept? In more than 120 stores, world-leading designers and manufacturers sell out of stock quantities of their production without damaging their name and prestige. Here you can buy original luxury goods with a discount of up to 70% of their price in the boutique of the same brand in the center of Lisbon or another world capital. Architecturally, Campera is built like a typical Portuguese town, with shady streets with orange trees, charming squares with cafes and restaurants with tables under the shade of oleanders. Every day there is a free bus to the center that leaves from Gare do Oriente.

CONCLUSION

In conclusion, "With Knife and Fork around the Globe" has taken us on a remarkable journey, not only through the tantalizing flavors and aromas of European cuisine but also into the intricate tapestry of anthropology, cultural diversity, and the rich history of food. Throughout our exploration of 12 captivating European countries, we have witnessed how food acts as a powerful lens, offering insights into the essence of a culture, its people, and the stories that have shaped their culinary traditions.

Anthropology has played a central role in our culinary odyssey, revealing the deep-rooted connections between food and human societies. We have discovered how the availability of local ingredients, geographical influences, and even climate have influenced the development of unique culinary identities. From the seafood-rich shores of Portugal to the hearty and robust dishes of Germany, each region's gastronomy has been shaped by its natural surroundings and the resourcefulness of its inhabitants.

Cultural diversity has been a guiding force throughout our journey, as we have savored the distinct flavors and techniques that define each country's culinary heritage. The amalgamation of traditions brought by conquerors, settlers, and immigrants has resulted in a fascinating fusion of culinary influences. We have witnessed the delicate balance of French refinement, the passionate embrace of Italian simplicity, and the harmonious blend of Eastern and Western flavors found in Croatia's cuisine. These diverse culinary traditions serve as a testament to the vibrant tapestry of cultures that have shaped Europe throughout history.

Food has also provided us with a gateway to the past, allowing us to trace the historical footprints left on European culinary landscapes. Traditional recipes passed down through generations tell stories of triumphs, struggles, and the ingenuity of those who adapted to changing circumstances. From the medieval influences on British cuisine to the Ottoman heritage found in Turkish dishes, the history of food unravels the complexities of European history, acting as a tangible link to the past.

As we conclude our culinary adventure, let us reflect on the profound impact of food beyond its mere sustenance. It is a powerful tool for cultural exchange, fostering connections and understanding among people from different backgrounds. It has the ability to transcend language barriers and unite individuals through the universal language of taste.

May this guide inspire you to continue your culinary explorations, to delve deeper into the intricate relationship between food and culture, and to savor every bite as a testament to the human spirit's ingenuity and creativity. As you embark on your own culinary journeys, remember that each plate carries a story, each bite opens a new chapter, and each shared meal is an opportunity to forge lasting connections.

Bon appétit, and may your culinary adventures continue to ignite a passion for discovery and a profound appreciation for the diverse flavors that make our world so extraordinary.

Don't miss out!

Visit the website below and you can sign up to receive emails whenever Mags Pie publishes a new book. There's no charge and no obligation.

https://books2read.com/r/B-A-KBUZ-UVJMC

BOOKS 2 READ

Connecting independent readers to independent writers.

Also by Mags Pie

All About Eggs
Dream Reader
With Knife & Fork Around the Globe
Fin, the Fish of Syllable Sea
Чудесаторът

www.ingramcontent.com/pod-product-compliance
Lightning Source LLC
Chambersburg PA
CBHW020257180726
47994CB00027B/898